The Really Practical Guide to Starting Up Your Own Business

Kim Hills Spedding

authorHOUSE®

AuthorHouse™ UK Ltd.
1663 Liberty Drive
Bloomington, IN 47403 USA
www.authorhouse.co.uk
Phone: 0800.197.4150

Second edition published by AuthorHouse 5/23/2013

ISBN: 978-1-4520-6156-6 (sc)
ISBN: 978-1-4817-8932-5 (e)

DEDICATION

This book is dedicated to my dear wife 'H', who encouraged me to write the book and who subsequently spent many hours and days helping to produce the manuscript ready for publishing.

PREFACE

You picked up, clicked on this book because you are thinking of starting your own business and really want someone to show you how to **actually** go about doing so? I have advised small businesses for over two and a half decades and in my experience, what people need is really practical advice. It's not the big ideas that entrepreneurs and potential business owners need. They mostly come up with those themselves, fuelled by the passion and commitment that they're going to need to succeed. It is the practical advice that people want to know and I have found very few books that provide it. This is why I have written this book. You can read any number of tomes on business theory, but **if what you are after is a really practical guide to take you through step by step all the things you need to consider and action then this book is for you!**

Throughout this book there is practical advice, tips and suggestions on every aspect of planning and starting up your own business.

I have run a business in this field for over 25 years, the first ten years running an Enterprise Agency in Oxford. Many of the suggestions are based on things my team and I did to ensure that we provided a sound basis and example for the 3,500 businesses we helped start up in Oxfordshire in that time. Since then, I have been a self employed independent business adviser/counsellor/mentor, giving one-to-one advice, as well as a trainer presenting Business Planning courses in Berkshire, Bedfordshire, Buckinghamshire, Hertfordshire and Oxfordshire, for both Pre-Start and Existing businesses.

As a business counsellor/adviser and a trainer over that whole time, I have been seeing people regularly who came to talk about this great idea they had to start up their own business, who all asked

'What would you do if you were me – how do I go about actually getting my business up and running?'

Many of the answers I gave them are here in this book.

The chapters in this book are set out in a logical order of the steps you will need to take. For example it is no good spending days and days designing a brochure or thinking you must have an office before you have gone through whether you should be doing this at all or until you have conducted your market research.

You will find that some chapters contain a repetition of advice, points made in an earlier chapter. This is because they need to be considered in the context of that chapter but are equally relevant and linked to another aspect and chapter. For example consideration of 'Features and Benefits' is a vital part of developing your Marketing strategy, but is of course equally vital to understand when Selling.

Lastly in looking at the index you may decide to avoid dealing with, say, the financial aspects as being in the 'too difficult to deal with' box. Have a go at reading these 'too difficult to deal with' chapters – they were written assuming 'nil knowledge' and in lay language. Whatever you do, don't just leave it and hope it will be all right on the day. Go and see a business counsellor/adviser at an Enterprise Agency/ Chamber of Commerce.

Kim Hills Spedding

TABLE OF CONTENTS

CHAPTER ONE

WHY DO YOU WANT TO START YOUR OWN BUSINESS?

There may be one or a number of reasons you have come to this decision:

- You have a great idea for a product or service.

- You have a saleable/buyable skill, which can earn you money

- You always came up with ways you could earn money when you were at school – Saturday jobs or maybe buying and selling things amongst your friends.

- You buy and sell things on '**e-bay**' and try out various ideas to make yourself a lot of money.

- Your parents run a successful business of their own.

- You have had enough of other people (parents, teachers) telling you how to run your life whilst still at home/school. You want to control your own destiny.

- You have been employed and feel you can do a far better job than your bosses. You don't want to go on earning them lots of money that you could make for yourself.

- You are unemployed and want to get off State benefits.

- You have always been employed and have reached mid-career and can't readily see the way ahead. Maybe you fear you are going to be made redundant at an age when you feel you will not be able to get another job easily.

- You have been made redundant or taken early retirement, you have plenty of steam left in you and need or would like to go on earning money.

- You have retired, have a pension and want to turn a hobby into a business.

IS SELF EMPLOYMENT REALLY FOR ME

It is vital to recognise that you are at a crossroads in your life

Before you consider going off down another road you need to ask yourself **FOUR QUESTIONS** as to whether self employment is really for you.

1. **Do I have the necessary skills/experience to do what I am thinking of doing?**

2. **Do I have the necessary attributes? Am I that sort of person?**

3. **Have I got enough money? Will I need to borrow?**

4. **Will I have the support of family and friends?**

1. *Do I have the necessary skills/experience to do what I am thinking of doing?*

You are going to be competing with other people already in business who do know how. If you have any doubts about this it is vital you get yourself on a training course and/or go to work for someone who does know how, to pick their brains and watch what they do. You can find out what training courses are available at your local library, or on the internet . Key in a subject and location to find out what is available, when and where and how to book, or contact your local Chamber of Commerce/Enterprise Agency/College of Further Education.

You may have a brilliant idea but do you have the necessary skills to run the business?

- Do you know how to plan and market your business?

- Do you know how to sell?

- Can you do your own book keeping?

- Do you understand what your accounts will be telling you about your financial state?

- Can you manage people?

- Are you good at managing your time?

Over the years I have seen many able people who had a particular skill or idea but who started a business without getting the training in the skills they needed to run the business.

They had a Business Plan when they started, but put it in a drawer once the bank had agreed the loan/overdraft. Any plan they then had was in their heads or they were running their business by instinct, by 'the seat of their pants'.

They employed others but tended to do most things themselves because it was quicker and easier for them to do so. They had developed their business to the extent of their innate abilities but could not take it any further. They told me about their large turnover but omitted to tell me that they had a huge overdraft and were not making a profit. They went to their office, shop or workspace unit and rushed around looking busy but were going nowhere, they were on a treadmill.

It is vital that you get training in the business skills you don't have before you start your business, and that you regularly review your Business Plan.

2. Do I have the necessary attributes? Am I that sort of person?

Ask yourself the following questions if self employment is to be your main source of income:

- **Am I prepared to work long hours?**

Being self employed is not a Monday to Friday, 9 to 5 existence. You will be knocking on the doors of people who might give you business and those who will say no thank you. Then when you get the business you have to do everything yourself.

- **Am I resilient?**

Things will be sent to challenge you, if you tend to give up easily, don't go into business.

- **Can I make decisions?**

When running your own business you will constantly need to make decisions. You cannot check with a boss, you are the boss. Many people go through life avoiding making decisions in case they make a mistake.

- **How good is my judgment?**

How well have you made major decisions in your life? Have you tended to get them right or wrong? How good have you been at judging people and situations?

- **Am I fit?**

When you are self-employed there is no Statutory Sick Pay (unless you are a Company Director) and customers will not pay you if you are not there to do the job.

- **Can I work alone?**

It is a very lonely existence being your own boss. Many people miss the camaraderie of working with others. There will be no one to encourage you when you are feeling low.

- **Can I blow my own trumpet, without sounding big headed?**

Most people are naturally modest and if you have always been employed you probably haven't needed to tell people how good you are. A tendency I have observed over the years is that people offer negative statements about what they cannot do as a defence mechanism. Never make negative statements about what you cannot do. If you are asked if you can do something, and you can't, say 'No I can't but I know someone who can' which will give you time to work out how you are going to deal with the problem.

Think positively. If you give out negative 'vibes' you are 'dead in the water'.

The last personal attribute which will help your survival out there is:

- **Have I got a bit of steel down my backbone?**

You have to be firm and strong. There are some very unscrupulous people you will be tempted to do business with, who will promise you the earth, then run up credit with you which they have no intention of paying. They have various ways of taking *advantage of unsuspecting newcomers to the market.*

3. Have I enough money? Will I need to borrow?

You may not need a lot of money to get started but your business is unlikely to generate sufficient income at first for you to live on**. You need to talk to a Business Bank Manager to** get their support during the early stages. **You may never have needed to talk to a bank manager before but do so now.** They recognise that your business will not generate enough income for some time but that you still have to eat and pay for your housing. They may help you with an overdraft but they will need to see your Business Plan and your Cash Flow Forecast.

If you need to borrow, the bank will only lend you money if you are putting in some of your own. You will also be working for the first few years for the bank, unless you are successful enough to be able to pay off the loan early from profits.

4. Will I have the support of family and friends?

Before emotion and fatigue set in it is vital to talk to people who are going to be affected by you starting up your own business, and about how it's all going to be for them. How:-

- **You have to work all hours**

- **You may get tired and irritable**

- **You won't be available for social life**

- **You probably won't be able to take holidays for the foreseeable future**

- One room or part of a room in the house has got to be the office as you must have somewhere you can leave your papers (don't try and work at the end of your kitchen or on the dining room table).

> **REALLY PRACTICAL TIP** But do tell them about the tremendous rewards if you get it right. Never again will you worry about being made redundant, or have to sign on regularly at the Job Centre. Tell them about the better things you might achieve in your life – to share with them.

You need to be totally focussed in developing your new business – you need everyone supporting and encouraging you.

SUMMARY

It is important that you ask yourself these **FOUR QUESTIONS,** and don't try to fix the answers.

If you are not this sort of a person, then don't start your own business!

It won't make you a lesser human being if you come to this conclusion – it might be a very sensible decision <u>not</u> to start a business, but to seek fulfilment in some other way.

Perhaps seeing your employed job as a means to an end and doing something with a hobby or working for a good cause to achieve the fulfilment you are looking for.

Between 50% and 70% of all the clients who came for advice, attended training courses in the various Enterprise Agencies, Chambers of Commerce I have worked in, went away and decided not to proceed with their business idea. This was not because we as counsellors or trainers said 'what a silly idea' or 'I don't think you are going to be able to make it' – but people went away and had a quiet think about these four questions

TO BE OR NOT TO BE SELF EMPLOYED?

If you have been put off by these questions then whatever you do –

DO NOT START YOUR OWN BUSINESS

Try selling this book to a friend, who is thinking of starting!

TAKE YOUR IDEA FORWARD - SEE AN ADVISER

The first thing you must do if you intend to go ahead with your idea to start a business is make an appointment to see a Business Counsellor/Adviser at an Enterprise Agency / Chamber of Commerce (Small Business Counselling Service). The local addresses are usually listed in **the Yellow Pages under 'Business Enterprise Agencies', 'Chambers of Commerce and Trade', 'National Enterprise Network'** or on the internet – **(www. britishchambers.org.uk), (www.nationalenterprisenetwork. org).** The appointments are generally free of charge and you will see someone who is experienced, non judgmental and able to talk to you in total confidence about your idea, the various courses of action you may like to consider, how to go about doing your market research, and how to gather the facts to put in your Business Plan. They may encourage you to go on training courses to learn how to put together a Business Plan and acquire other skills you will need to run the business. They may also signpost you to other people who can help such as accountants, solicitors, banks.

You can see the Business Counsellor/Adviser for free as often as you wish to get the Business Plan together, to have it challenged before you go to ask the Bank for the money, sign a lease, or before starting up.

CHAPTER TWO

PLANNING THE BUSINESS

Most people when told they need to put together a Business Plan to start up their own business claim they don't know how to plan - they just want to start up.

But of course we all know how to plan because we do it in our daily lives – if we are doing a big shop we make a list – that's a plan; if we are going on holiday we get information from the internet or go to a travel agent to ensure that we have thought of all the aspects, where we are going, how we are going to get there, when, what to take, packing, what money we need, and so forth – we PLAN.

PLANNING A BUSINESS IS NO DIFFERENT. THERE ARE A LOT OF THINGS YOU NEED TO FIND OUT, BUT IT IS NOT ROCKET SCIENCE – JUST PLAIN COMMON SENSE!

The success of your business depends on knowing

- **where you are**
- **where you want to be**
- **how to get there**

The Business Plan is your Road Map

Before you make a new journey by car you key in your destination on 'sat nav', or you look at a map and regularly check as you go along to see that you are not losing your way. Starting off in business is no different. You must think carefully about what you are setting out to do, write it down and seek all the advice and gather all the facts you can get. The very act of writing it down and producing a

Business Plan will help you think through all aspects which have to be considered.

Talking to an independent Business Counsellor and having them challenge your Business Plan, before asking the Bank for a loan or using your own savings, will ensure you have, on paper, a reasonable chance of success.

Once started, it is important to see your **Business Plan as a blueprint** for what you think you can achieve and **as a benchmark** to see how you actually do against what you estimated you would do. **It should not be put in the bottom drawer and forgotten**. The Business Plan puts all the information you need to obtain and consider into a logical, ordered format which will allow you to assess the implications or look for weaknesses.

Once your business is up and running it will tell you when things are not going according to plan, in time for you to take action. It is particularly important to check regularly as to whether you are making a profit or not, to be able to take action to work faster, reduce costs, put up your prices, or maybe a combination of some or all of these factors.

Just because there is money in the bank does not mean you are making a profit.

You cannot possibly produce a Business Plan which then happens exactly as expected, but if you have done thorough research, and constantly refer to it, any deviations will be minor and easily fixed.

It will need to be updated from time to time in the light of actual experience of trading, so always date your plan.

So you need a Format

BUSINESS PLAN FORMATS

Each of the High Street Banks provides a Business Start Up Pack, with a Business Plan Format, which you may wish to use, particularly if you are going to ask them for money. These can be downloaded from their web sites or obtained direct from banks. Enterprise Agencies, Small Business Counselling Services provided by Chambers of Commerce, usually have their own format which can be downloaded from their web sites (see Useful Addresses/Contacts at the back of the book).

All formats contain these main elements:-

- **The Idea for the Business**

- **The Aims and Objectives – Personal/Business**

- **Description of Product/Service**

- **Findings of Market Research**

- **Marketing Plan**

- **Selling Method**

- **Premises and Equipment**

- **Finance**
  Capital Requirement
  Sales Forecasts
  Cash Flow/Profit and Loss Forecasts
  Book Keeping

- **Legal Aspects**
  Structures
  Protection
  -name
  -idea
  -terms of trade
  -employment
  -premises
  -insurance
  -health and safety
  -data protection
  -employing people

- **Skills – Own/Business**

- **S.W.O.T. (Strengths and Weaknesses, Opportunities, Threats) Analysis**

The Idea for the Business

It is important to consider all the options you may have in starting a business, including harnessing your years of experience gained whilst employed. Many people I have seen over the years completely disregarded that experience because they were tired of the 'rat race', thought only in terms of being employed in their field, felt that they couldn't 'cold call'. But in this day and age when firms are contracting out many of their activities previously done in house, there are many opportunities for experienced people in a self employed capacity to offer their services as consultants, trouble shooters, or project managers. Look at all your ideas, gather the information and assess the relative merits, before deciding on which option you are going to progress.

> **REALLY PRACTICAL TIP** Put your drive to be gainfully employed into neutral whilst you consider all your options. Don't go for the first 'apple on the tree - you need to see what else there is in the orchard'.

Aims and Objectives

It is important to consider, and write down what it is you are seeking to achieve from starting a business – **what are your personal long term aims** and what do you need to do in **the shorter term (your objectives)** to help you **achieve the long term aim**.

Are you doing this

- For fulfilment?
- To survive?
- To supplement some other form of income?
- To have better things in life?
- To have an independent source of income?
- To become very wealthy?

Doing this is also the beginning of **time management,** to remind you where you are headed and to ask yourself as you work away whether what you are currently doing is helping you get to where you want to be. (See Chapter 14 – Other Considerations.)

The **main aim of your business** is probably to generate sufficient income to **achieve your most important personal aim**. It might also be to develop your business to the extent that you can sell it at a later date and retire.

The **shorter term objectives of your business** are to set yourself targets towards achieving your longer term aim and to have a system to monitor your progress (to keep and scrutinise records).

There is a mnemonic, S.M.A.R.T., to assess your business objectives:-

- **S**pecific – e.g. a 20% increase in sales by, say, July
- **M**easurable – you need to keep records and know whether you hit the target
- **A**chievable – they are not beyond your ability or reach
- **R**ealistic – they are not too high or too low
- **T**ime based – you set a deadline, e.g. by a certain date

Your Ability/Previous Experience/Skills

You may be the greatest exponent of your particular business idea in your area, but do you have the other skills you will need to run it as a business?

You may have held a senior management position in a company where you could rely on other people to complement your skills or ability who were experts in their field.

If you are going to be a Sole Trader, only Director when you first start you will need to have a variety of skills in addition to your occupational skills, for example administration, marketing/sales, planning, book keeping, financial management, people management, time management, communication skills.

Identify those areas by doing a Strength and Weakness analysis on your skills. Where you need training, plan to attend courses to acquire or improve business management skills– **before** you start your business. (See Chapter 14 – SWOT Analysis.)

BUSINESS PLAN – Title Page

You need to put a summary of your plan on the front cover/title page.

This should state:

- **The Name of the business**
- **The Address/Telephone/E-mail address**
- **Your Title, e.g. Owner, Partner, Director**
- **Legal Status**
- **Description of the Business**
- **Name of Accountant and Solicitor**
- **Bank Account**
- **Finance Required**

Business Name

Have a name for your business which makes an impact. It should explain what you do and project a quality image. You can use your own name, particularly if you have built a reputation whilst being employed and you are remaining in the same field.

Avoid using the same name as an existing business as they could take you to court for a 'passing off' action. (See Chapter 8 - Legal Aspects - Protecting the Business - Business Names.) Check in the Yellow Pages in the area you will operate.

Check also with Companies House (www.companieshouse.gov.uk), as to whether an existing company is using the name. You cannot use the same name even if you are not intending to become a company. There are restrictions on the use of certain words. There is guidance on the Companies House web site.

If you plan to operate beyond your local area check with the website (www.anewbusiness.co.uk) to see if you have chosen the same name as an existing Sole Trader, Partnership or Company. This site is maintained by Business Names Registration Ltd. and lists all those businesses (including Sole Traders and Partnerships) who have registered with them but is not exhaustive. If you find that there is another firm using the same name but in a totally different part of the country, check as to whether they have any objections. They/ you may be planning to remain local and therefore not compete.

You cannot register your name as a Sole Trader or Partnership to protect it from being used by others, but there are other ways. (See Chapter 8.)

Business Address/Premises

You will probably start your business by working from home. You may alternatively use 'Serviced Office Accommodation' or have to rent premises. Each option has advantages and disadvantages which you will need to consider in order to make the right decision before you have your stationery or sales literature printed. (See Chapter 6 - Premises.)

Legal Status

You have to adopt a legal structure for your business. There are a number to choose from:-

- **Sole Trader**
- **Partnership**

- **Limited Liability Partnership**

- **Limited Company**

You need to consider the **Advantages and Disadvantages of each**, to ascertain which will best suit you. (See Chapter 7 – Legal Structures.)

Accountant and Solicitor – Professional Advice

As part of your preparation to start a business it is important to take professional advice from an Accountant and/or Solicitor.

You will need to talk to **an Accountant** (initial session should be free) to find out:

- What records (books) you need to keep?

- How to legally minimise your tax liabilities, what you can set against your income?

- When you should complete your first period of trading (most suggest you tie in with the tax year and have a 31st March year end)?

- What it will cost to pull together your first year's accounts and do the Tax Return?

The other consideration is whether you get on with the Accountant. He or she should become a good friend and supporter of your business. You also need to ask them what the fees will be and do they also offer advice. Some just do the number crunching.

Contact the Institute of Chartered Accountants (www.chartered-accountants.co.uk) to get a list of local Accountants, or your Bank Manager, Enterprise Agency, Chamber of Commerce may be able to give you some names based locally.

You may need to talk to **a Solicitor** if you are:

- Setting up a Partnership (a Partnership Agreement)

- Setting up a Limited Company

- Entering into contracts with customers (Terms and Conditions of Trading)

- Taking on Premises (looking at leases)
- Taking on Staff

The Law Society (www.lawsociety.org.uk) operates a scheme known as 'Lawyers for your Business', whereby a Solicitor will see people free for an initial half hour session. Not all solicitor practices subscribe to the Scheme so check before you make an appointment. Contact the Law Society for Solicitors locally involved with the scheme.

Bank Account

You will need to open up a separate business bank account to run your business. Do not muddle up your domestic and business finances in one account.

Business Bank accounts are normally offered with a free period of banking at the start, but then attract higher bank charges than a domestic account.

Some Building Societies/Banks offer free business banking but the services offered are possibly not as comprehensive as those who do charge.

If you form a Limited Company you will need your 'Certificate of Incorporation' to open the account. Banks will require Personal Guarantees from Company Directors for loans made to the Company.

SUMMARY

So, having decided on a name for your business, where you are going to operate, what your objectives are, what skills you will need and the vital importance of a Business Plan, you are ready to start doing the work to put together your Plan.

BUT before you go any further you also need to consider the following:-

Reasons Why Businesses Fail

In this country surveys are done every couple of years by one or more of the Banks, which show that:

One in three businesses fail in their first year of trading.

There are a number of reasons why this happens:

- Some people decide it is **too much like hard work and give up.**

- Some decide to **go back to employment, or are offered a job** when visiting businesses to do their research.

- **Overestimating Sales**

You need to be optimistic to start up your own business, but you also have to be realistic. It is highly unlikely that your business will start generating sales and income at the rate you need or expect from day one.

It could take one to three years to reach your full potential. So it is important to be realistic in your sales forecasts and to talk to your Business Bank Manager about the need for overdraft support in the early months, unless you have funds of your own to draw on for 'working capital' i.e. your monthly cash flow needs, to cover the replenishment of stocks, giving of credit and your own drawings/ salary. (See Chapter 10 - Financial Planning - 'How to do your Sales Forecasts'.)

- **Underestimating Costs**

Many people guess at what it is going to cost, or underestimate the number of things they are going to have to spend money on. This results in wrong pricing, or they run out of money, or need to find additional funds – which puts a different complexion on the viability of the venture. (See Chapter 3 - Costs and Chapter 4 – Pricing.)

- **Failure to Control Costs**

In starting and running a business there is likely to be a lot of expenditure. If this is being met from personal savings and/or redundancy money there may be a temptation to buy resources in excess of your initial needs which may bring higher overhead and running costs. It is vital to watch every aspect of your costs.

- **Losing Control of Cash Flow**

You may be tempted to buy lots of stock at a 'bargain' price. Maybe it is nearly obsolete or past its 'sell by' date. Ask your supplier how long it takes to get stock to you. It is better to get it 'just in time' to supply your customer.

You may not like to press your new customers for payment who may take full advantage of your 'soft attitude' to fund their cash flow and delay paying you. If too many do that you will go out of business.

- **Inadequate Market Research**

To fully research your business idea will take a great deal of time and effort if it is to be done properly.

Many people just do a bit or talk to their friends and family, who tell them what a wonderful idea it is. You may know of someone else doing what you are thinking of doing and making a lot of money and so you may feel you can just start up and hope it will all work.

You will have seen shops in your local town that opened and closed within the first year because they did not take the simple step of sitting outside the premises they were thinking of taking at different times of the day, days of the week, times of the year to do a 'footfall' count. (i.e. to count how many people walked past the premises, stopped and visited). Were there going to be enough people spending enough money to be able to make a success of the business?

They could have worked out how much money they needed each day just to cover the overheads. Doing the sums could have saved them from signing a lease for a business that was never going to cover its costs. *I have seen people who were still paying rent on premises a number of years after the business stopped trading.*

Landlords don't let you off – 'Didn't your business work – oh dear'!

- **Failing to Meet Customer's Needs**

The key to starting up a successful business is to have identified what your potential customers 'need'. This can only be established by talking to a representative sample of potential customers. Many people just talk to a few, or think they know, or get answers they don't want to hear and proceed anyway.

IT IS VITAL TO TALK TO POTENTIAL CUSTOMERS AND MORE IMPORTANTLY TO LISTEN TO WHAT THEY ARE TELLING YOU THEY NEED.

I once saw a lady who had spent two years sending out mail shots telling local people about her wonderful idea. She had also spent £3000 on a web site. I had a look at her mail shots and web site which listed the features of what she had to offer but made no mention of the benefits.

I asked her if she had ever been out to talk to potential customers about whether they shared her view that her idea was something they wanted. 'No' she said, she had not talked to anyone!

- **Insufficient Range of Business Skills**

Some people start up their business with a particular skill or idea, but don't have time to acquire the other business skills they need. They develop their business to the extent of their innate abilities but can't get any further.

It is vital to acquire the other skills you will need to manage all aspects of the business before you start. At first you will not be able to afford to buy in resources to help you.

- **Taking Unnecessary Risks**

Many people fail because they just **take a 'flyer' and trust to luck.** There is no substitute to gathering lots of facts, talking to as many potential customers as possible, and then **taking 'calculated' risks** armed with lots of information.

- **Under pricing**

Starting your business by being the cheapest is not the only way to get business but you will soon go out of business as your competitors, who have greater reserves, drop their prices to put you, the newcomer, out of business. (See Chapter 4 – Pricing.)

- **Failure to Plan**

Again, people who don't need to borrow money or are quite convinced they are on to a winner and can just start up, don't bother with a Business Plan.

It is vital to ensure, by producing a Business Plan, that your venture will be the best use of your own savings or redundancy award or money borrowed from a bank, family or friends.

OVERALL

- **People committing to a Course of Action that is not fully understood.**

Many of these factors can be avoided or overcome if you, the Business Owner, are prepared for them.

THAT IS WHY A BUSINESS PLAN IS SO IMPORTANT

Assuming that you feel you can do what is necessary to avoid making the same mistakes

WHAT NEXT?

Well, the heart of your Business Plan is the information you need to gather in carrying out the Market Research to arrive at a Marketing Strategy which then needs to be translated into the income this will generate, other costs it will incur and the likely profits.

The Plan will also need to consider the resources – people, equipment and the money you will need to implement your strategy, to get your business started. It will also need to consider Legal and other Financial aspects.

CHAPTER THREE

MARKET RESEARCH

You may think you have come up with the greatest idea for starting a business. Your family and friends tell you it can't fail. You may know of someone already running a similar business in another part of the country, or perhaps a franchise operation which is making a fortune. You may be right in your assumptions, but:

- until you venture out into the particular area you want to trade in and **talk to potential customers** about what you have in mind and **listen to what they are telling you they need**

- until you have found out all you can about **what it is going to cost**, to start up and then operate

- until you amass as much information you can **about your competitors**, including their strengths and weaknesses, **you are going to be taking a huge risk and are likely to fail.**

If you are lucky by nature then of course just go ahead and do it, but if you are not, there are no short cuts. **Talking and listening to as many people as possible, gathering a huge mass of facts, and then writing it all down in a Business Plan is what has to be done.**

You need to carry out Market Research from two sources:

- **Desk Research**

  - Looking up and reading published information

- **Field Research**
  - Customers
  - Customer Reaction/Needs
  - Costs
  - Competition

You may be a gregarious outgoing person who would rather skimp the **desk research** and get out there talking to people, looking at what goes on in the market place – the **field research.**

You might be someone who prefers to look up information online or in a book – **desk research.**

Both types of research need to be done

DESK RESEARCH

The first step is to carry out Desk Research, because much of the information is readily accessible at little or no cost. The statistics may indicate that overall trade in the market sector you are considering entering is increasing year on year, in excess of inflation – **it is a 'growing' market.** They may, however, show the opposite trend – **a 'declining' market.** Information gathered in this way is known as 'secondary' data. It is basically accessing and assimilating relevant published information.

Where to Look?

- **Internet**

Using Search Engines like 'Google', 'Yahoo', 'Wikipedia' will provide you with vast amounts of published information (website addresses are shown in the various categories listed).

Logging into Social Media Networks such as 'LinkedIn' (www. linkedin.com), 'Facebook' (www.facebook.com), will enable you to communicate with other people (potential customers), as will 'Twitter' and Blogs. Properly targeted these can increase your exposure, whilst reducing your marketing expenditure without losing impact. (Ask Enterprise Agencies, Banks, Libraries for a copy of the' Business

Information Fact Sheet No. 467 – An Introduction to Social Media for Business', from the Cobweb Information series).

- **Library – Business Reference Section**

Make this your next port of call. There is a team of very knowledgeable Business Reference Librarians, who can tell you what is available and how to access the information held by the Library, either in hard copy form – e.g. directories, or on the internet – databases, market sector reports, etc.

- **Professional/Trade Associations**

If you already belong to an Association, continue your membership. This will give you access to their publications and meetings, to keep you up to speed on your subject and to enable you to meet up with others – to network. If you are not a member, consider joining – you might also get other benefits such as lower Professional Indemnity Insurance premiums. (See Chapter 8 – Legal Aspects - Protecting the Business.)

- **Chamber of Commerce**

Some Chambers have their own Resource Centre or Library which can be readily accessed, even if you are not a member. They hope you'll join by seeing the information and other services they can offer members.

- **Companies House**

Every company in the U.K. has to lodge with Companies House the details of its Accounts, the names of the Directors, their addresses, their dates of birth and what other directorships they hold or have held.

It is your right to have access to this information for any Company you are considering dealing with. Companies House will provide the information for a fee, but you can look up some of this information on the internet or in directories like '**Kompass' or 'Key British Enterprises'**. You need to check whether you are dealing with capable people and sound businesses. What is their track record with any companies they may have been involved with – are they incompetent or out to 'con' unsuspecting new businesses?

- **Local Authority – Development and Planning, Licensing, Environmental Health Departments**

If you are thinking of **taking premises**, check with the appropriate Local Authority to find out whether you need planning permission or change of use. Don't just take the word of the landlord or estate agent. If you are starting a business involving **selling food or drink, check with the Environmental Health Department.** You will need to satisfy them as to where and how you will be storing, preparing and delivering your products. You will also need to undertake some training in the hygienic handling of food if you are not already qualified in this field.

You need **licences** for certain types of business – nursing homes, taxi services, food, drink and catering – contact the Licensing Department. (See also Chapter 8 – Legal Aspects - Protecting the Business.)

You can look up **Planning Applications**, usually advertised in the local paper, to offer your services to homeowners, builders, architects for building work or landscape gardening.

What to Look at?

- **Telephone Directories, Yellow Pages, Thompson Directories** These will give you names, addresses and telephone numbers

- **Trade Directories**

Most Local Authorities produce Trade Directories listing all the businesses in their area who pay business rates or have asked to be included. Details are also provided of the Industrial Trading Estates in the area by some Authorities.

Chambers of Commerce also produce a Directory of their members.

- **Dun and Bradstreet** produce a number of Business Directories which can be accessed at Libraries for free but online you have to register :-

- **'Key British Enterprises'** – giving details of all Companies, their communication information, their directors, basic financial information such as turnover and year end results, what they do and how many staff they employ. They also provide a financial risk indicator.

- **'Euro Pages'** – a Directory of European businesses

- 'Who Owns Whom' – U.K. and Continental Europe – a directory of Parent Company/Subsidiary information.

• **'Kompass'** directories list details of all U.K. Companies. The information can be accessed by county, town or by market sector, and lists similar information to Key British Enterprises.

• **'Willings Press Guide'** – a directory of British publications.

• **'Benn's Media'** – a directory of all other media.

• **Government Statistics** - available either in hard copy form from Libraries or on the internet – (www.ons.gov.uk). This will give you statistics on market trends.

• **Socio-Economic Population statistics** – available in hard copy form from Libraries or on the internet. www.ons.gov.uk - click on 'People and Places'. The site will give you a profile of the population, by age, marital status, ethnicity, lifestyle, and much more. This will enable you to determine, for example, how many people there are in the area who are likely to be your target market for your product or service.

• **Electoral Register** - you can view this at a Local Authority office, or a main post office. This will give you the name of a householder against an address, unless they have ticked the 'non publication' box when completing their Electoral Roll questionnaire. This could be used to personalise mail shots, leaflet drops.

• **National, Local, Business Newspapers/Journals**

Reading newspapers and journals will present you with opportunities to identify potential business.

For example, the '**Engagement' columns** will provide information on who is getting married, and could be targeted by those providing a range of services for weddings.

- **Information on Planning Applications** will give those providing services like building, plumbing, painting, decorating, electrical work, garden and interior design, etc., an opportunity to contact the householder, developer, architect to explore opportunities to provide a quotation.

- **New legislation** will provide opportunities to provide services to enable businesses or the public to obey the law.

- **Businesses advertising for 'part time staff'** could be approached to explore whether they have considered using people on a 'self employed' basis, thus saving on NI costs. The person providing such services would have to work for at least one other firm, to avoid being classified as an employee.

- **Telephoning all your competitors who advertise in the local newspaper**, to see 'how soon could they do your (theoretical) job'. If they all say tomorrow, is there room for one more business? If they say there is a 'waiting list' then there is room for your business.

Doing a bit of lateral thinking on information you read in newspapers will usually present you with opportunities to get business. Every newspaper has a '**Wanted' column** – could you provide what is 'wanted'?

- **Company Reports and Accounts** – gives more detailed information than 'Kompass'. Ring the Company to ask for a copy – say you are thinking of 'using them', 'buying shares', 'going to work for them', etc.!

- **Competitors' Literature** – ask them to send you their details, price lists using the same excuses as above. Look up their web site.

- **'Business Opportunity Profiles' and 'Business Information Fact Sheets'**

These are a series of very useful information packed sheets published by Cobweb Information Ltd. in Gateshead, which you can obtain from your Local Enterprise Agency, Chamber of Commerce, most Banks and Libraries. You cannot download them on to your printer from the Internet, unless you subscribe to the service. (Tel no: 0191 461 8000, e-mail info@cobwebinfo.com.)

This may seem like a lot of reading when you just want to get on and start. You perhaps prefer just to go and talk to people or observe what goes on out in the 'market place'.

Some people I've met over the years didn't want to hear the 'too difficult to deal with' bits. They just wanted to start.

SUMMARY

Desk Research is an essential part of Market Research, but you also need **first hand or 'primary' data**, obtained by carrying out **'field research'**. Although more time consuming and costly, this is the only way to obtain an accurate and up to date picture of the potential market for your new business and should help to confirm the information you gleaned in your Desk Research.

FIELD RESEARCH

It will not be enough to read published information on internet or hard copy, fill your Business Plan with a lot of statistics and assume your business will be a success.

You also need to go out into '**the field', the 'market place'** to talk and listen to real live **potential customers**, to find out what everything will **cost** and to find out as much as you can about the people who are trading already – your **competitors.**

THE MAIN AREAS FOR FIELD RESEARCH ARE

- **Customers**
- **Customer Needs/Reaction to your idea**
- **Costs**
- **Competition**

Customers

Who are your potential customers? Are they members of the public, other businesses, firms or organisations? Who might 'signpost' people to you?

Are your potential customers from more than one sector of the population or sector of the business market? This is known as '**segmentation**' but as a small business it is better to start your business by concentrating on a few types of customer. You cannot be all things to all people!

You need to compile a list and then go and talk to a representative sample of potential customers/sign posters. You can't talk to all your likely customers, but you must approach a large enough 'sample'.

- Think about what information you need (on which you can base decisions) and develop a 'questionnaire' to provide that information.

- Define who is likely to have the information, e.g. different sectors of the population, other businesses, suppliers, trade associations, organisations.

- Consider different survey methods and the size of your sample.

Sampling

Select a representative sample from each group. It is important that each sample is large enough to provide meaningful information. The more you survey the more precise your information will be and the less chance that results are distorted by one respondent (whose answer may be incorrect or deliberately misleading).

It is suggested that a survey of about 150 would be an optimum sample for questioning members of the public with a Market Research Questionnaire, depending on the size of the population in the area you plan to trade in and range of potential customers.

You don't need to do more because if you carried out 1500 or 15000 individual interviews you would get a similar pattern of replies. We human beings tend to behave in given patterns.

If you do less or just ask friends then you may get a distorted picture.

It is your business. Do the interviews personally.

> **REALLY PRACTICAL TIP** Consider noting people's Body Language by putting a Code* on the bottom of each questionnaire, to help when you come to do your Sales Forecasts. What they were saying to you might be quite different from what their body language was telling you.

*V.E. - Very Enthusiastic   **Q.I.** - Quite Interested   **B.S**. - Bored Stiff

When you are looking at your 150 questionnaires some time after the interviews you won't remember the mix of the body language reaction.

What percentage were: V.E.   Q.I.   B.S.

> **REALLY PRACTICAL TIP** You won't be able to note people's body language if you rely solely on information gathered through a Social Networking site. There is nothing to beat getting in front of real people.

As regards **businesses/organisations, aim to see about 20% of potential customers.**

Survey Methods

Decide on the best way to obtain the information, weighing up the costs against the benefits.

Advantages and Disadvantages of Different Survey Methods

- **Mailed questionnaire** - high coverage at low cost, but low response, use suggested format below.

- **E-mailed questionnaires** - you can buy e-mail lists but check track record of supplier and understand the law on sending unsolicited e-mails to private individuals, use suggested format below.

- **Telephone survey** - quick but may not reach the right person.

- **Personal visits** - in-depth interviews possible, but expensive and time consuming, but this will produce the best information.

- **Street interviews** - use the market research multiple choice questionnaire (see suggested format below), note peoples' body language – time consuming, but probably the most effective method.

- **Personal observation** - counting the number of people who walk past/visit a shop if considering taking premises – 'footfall'.

The method – or mix of methods – you use will depend on your type of potential customer.

General Public

Is everyone out there a potential customer or just certain types of people, age groups, socio-economic groups?

Think about where members of the general public (those likely to be your potential customers) live or congregate. Are they at schools, playgroups, shopping centres, car parks, sports meetings, etc.? Then decide on the best means of obtaining the information.

Remember people out and about are usually intent on going somewhere, doing something else and are likely to be in a hurry when answering questions. So choose a time, perhaps at weekends or at lunchtime.

If, for example, you are planning to start a business making things which people would buy from shops, think about approaching people you see coming out of shops that are selling similar items, but don't stand immediately outside a shop – they will probably move you on!

Alternatively, you may have to approach people in their homes, over the telephone or through social networking sites.

Designing a Market Research Questionnaire

You will need a structured, multiple choice questionnaire for talking to, e-mailing members of the public – with no more than 8 to 10 questions. Do not ask questions where you have to write down their answers longhand. Just use a series of tick boxes with a range of choices beyond, but including, what you want to provide.

Make an opening statement when stopping members of the public to ask them if they mind answering some questions. Do not make a specific statement of what you are considering doing as this will condition their minds to giving you answers they think you want to hear. Rather, make a general statement that you 'are conducting a local survey into the demand for the provision of your types of products and / or services – and would they mind if you asked them a few questions?

Suggested Questions you should ask

- Your **first question** should be to establish, whether they have needed, wanted, bought these types of products/services **in the past** – yes or no. If Yes, who did they get them from and what did they think of the service?

- Then establish whether these are products/services they are likely to need, or want to buy **into the future** – if **Yes** ask an **ancillary question** listing the **range of different things they may need or want**.

- Your next question should seek to establish **the timing** and/ or **frequency** of demand for the different products/services. You may need a matrix offering options.

- Your next question is to establish what **price** they would expect to pay, offering a matrix of differing price levels for different products/services, reflecting the minimum/maximum price ranges for similar items already in the market.

- Your next question should seek to establish **the degree of importance they attach to other factors** which may influence their decision to buy from one supplier or another.

These could include: range available, quality, price, service, ease of access, distance from home, recommendations, attitude of staff/customer service. – Rate importance from '1 – not important' to '10 – extremely important'.

- Your **last question** should ask them for their **name, tel. no., e-mail, address**.

Your last question can only be asked if the person seems genuinely interested in what you have been talking about. This will give you your first potential customers if you contact them to 'give them an invitation to your grand opening' or a 'discount on their first purchase'. This will also enable you to telephone people who showed real interest, to do a second in-depth questionnaire.

Make sure your questions give you 'need to know' information rather than 'nice to know', or opinions. The questions should be so worded that people don't give you answers they think you want to hear!

Remember to note peoples' body language (see earlier comments under 'Sampling').

REALLY PRACTICAL TIP To give yourself a really professional Market Research Questionnaire consider looking up a website (www. surveymonkey.com) incorporating the suggested questions listed above.

Approaching Businesses and Organisations

Think about which types of companies or organisations are likely to be interested in buying your product/service.

Identify from Yellow Pages or Business Directories such as 'Kompass' the name, address and telephone number of potential clients/customers.

Telephone to find out the name of the 'decision maker' – the person you need to get in front of, who can make the decision. Find out how to spell their name, all their initials and their title/position in the business. Do not ask to be put through - they will be busy with other things on their mind.

The reason for getting this information is that, when you telephone to try to get an appointment, you will probably be asked to send your details, your literature, anything but agreeing there and then to giving you an appointment.

Use a letter or e-mail, properly addressed with the correct spelling, title and all initials, to get in front of the 'decision maker'.

> **REALLY PRACTICAL TIP** Just addressing it to 'The Manager' or 'Managing Director' will signal that you can't be bothered to find out the detail – that you are a 'broad brush' operator. They won't want to deal with someone signalling that attitude!

Your letter or e-mail should be no longer than one paragraph followed by two sentences. You are writing to busy people.

The **first paragraph** should set out what you have to offer, spelling out your experience, expertise in the products/services you have to offer. Mention the names of people you may have dealt with in the firm, in the past, when you were employed. 'Blow your trumpet' about any things you have done in your career of which you are particularly proud.

The **following sentence** should say 'how you would very much like the opportunity to come and talk to them about how your product/ service, expertise, experience, could '**benefit their business'**.

The **last sentence** should say 'I will telephone you in the next day or two to make an appointment'. **Do not say 'if you are interested, please ring me'.** Why should someone who is very busy call you, unless the moment your letter/e-mail lands on their desk/ screen it is something they need. If it isn't they will 'bin' your letter, delete your e-mail.

The use of a 'Tick Box' questionnaire when visiting businesses, firms or organisations is not appropriate. They will say 'my secretary could have done it over the phone'.

You will need to think through a framework of information you need to gather. You may need to talk to the PA/Secretary to convince them of the 'benefits' of their boss seeing you, or you may have to send a copy of your letter by e-mail directly to the person you want to deal with, by-passing the secretary, but most know how to filter-out unwanted callers. You may have to be persistent if you cannot get a date in the near future. Providing you do not make a nuisance of yourself, such as ringing daily, most people will eventually see you.

> **REALLY PRACTICAL TIP Once in front of the right person, remember you are there for four reasons. You are in 'market research mode'. NOT trying to get a sale on that first visit.**

If you go to see people and they think you are trying to sell them something they will 'put up the shutters' and you will achieve neither information nor a sale on that first visit.

These are the 4 reasons:

- **to tell them you exist**

- **to glean information about their business and future plans**

- **to sell yourself**

- **to find out what they need**

To tell them you exist – have a business card, which gives them your name, contact details including address, telephone/mobile number, e-mail address and on the back a list of bullet points of all the things you have to offer or are capable of doing. Do not give yourself a title or have a logo – these are 'market research mode' cards to give to people, from whom you hope to get information.

You could end up with cards with titles and a logo for a business you then don't run.

You are there to glean information about their likely future needs – it is unlikely they will want what you have in mind on the day you visit. In fact they will probably see you as a nuisance on two counts – they have got to stop doing whatever they are doing to listen to you and secondly they will see the '£' signs in your eyes – you are after their money.

Get them talking about their organisation, their plans, their problems – the subject they know best. Massage their ego, ask questions which may move them out of their 'comfort zone', maybe there is a better way of doing things – your way, which they had not considered before.

Make lots of notes, for three reasons:

Firstly, you will not remember what people told you when you have been to see a lot of different firms and organisations.

Secondly, you will be able to recall the details of your discussions some time after the event, when you telephone to 'fertilise' the seed you sowed when in front of them.

And **lastly,** you are signalling to people 'I am really interested in what you are telling me. I want to do business with you'. **Not making notes will signal to them that they are boring you – they may be, but make notes anyway!**

Be certain to ask them about their problem areas, do they have a budget available, and most importantly <u>when</u> do they expect to address the problem and put it out to tender for solution.

> **REALLY PRACTICAL TIP Diarise the date and get back to them a month before they plan to do something about it. This way you can better plan your diary and give yourself the opportunity to get there before the competition.**

The only thing you should be selling, on this first visit, is yourself.

We all make decisions in life to like someone or buy from them, often within seconds of meeting them. We then have that judgement confirmed or confounded by the way they then go on to speak or conduct themselves.

When you meet someone in a business environment you should be demonstrating by your questioning that you are competent, are a person who does what they say they will do – you are someone they can trust. If you are meeting someone you have dealt with before, remember they may not realise you have other competencies – they only had experience of one aspect of your abilities. Your range of questioning should demonstrate the extent of your competencies.

I had a guy come on a Mentoring course a few years ago who had been really successful and had vast experience as an employee in the Communications Industry. He had offered his services as a Mentor to help others. He had set up his own Communications business in the previous six months and mentioned in his opening introduction that it was not going as well as he had expected. At the refreshment break I asked him whether when he went in to see potential customers, including past clients he was always hoping to get a sale on that first visit - 'yes' he said – 'that's the problem' I suggested. At the end of the course he came up to me and agreed that piece of advice alone had been worth attending the course.

Lastly, you are there to find out what they need– not what you think they need, or what you want to do.

That is the key to your success – to provide what they need and at a profit.

Practical Suggestions for doing your Market Research

For some of the main types of businesses people start up there are common sense things you can do, by talking to and listening to people, reading readily available newspapers and publications, and thinking laterally.

- **Reading your local newspapers or national newspapers or trade journals**, can provide you with opportunities to gain business :-

For businesses providing any sort of household services, such as building, maintenance, electrical, plumbing, home security, gardening, by following up the Planning Application Notices published weekly. You can, as a member of the public look at the details in the Local Planning office and can then contact the house owner, builder, architect, to ask for an opportunity to quote, or to visit to discuss.

Similarly for these types of businesses, you can talk to the staff at Builders Merchants, to ask them to identify owner builders, who come in first thing in the morning to pick up the materials for the day's jobs. Introduce yourself and say you are looking for sub-contract work and could you meet them to explore possible work.

- **Cultivate your local Estate Agents**, who might **signpost** people, who have just moved in to the area, who may need the sort of services you provide. Leave a supply of your cards.

- **Ring up your competitors offering similar services** and ask them how soon they could do your repair/maintenance job. If they all say in the next couple of days, is there really room for one more business like yours?

- **For businesses providing wedding services, like catering, flowers, photography, car hire, dress/suit hire, musical entertainment, venues,** follow up announcements in newspapers of peoples' Engagements (where they are reasonably local, and have names which can be easily identified from telephone directories).

Write a letter congratulating them on their forthcoming wedding and ask to meet to discuss an opportunity to quote. Ask other businesses providing complementary services to **signpost** people – reciprocal trade.

- **Reading National newspapers or Trade Journals you may see reports of new legislation**, which businesses have to comply with which will give you the opportunity to approach all firms likely to be affected, for example new Health and Safety legislation.

- **Look up job advertisements where firms are looking to recruit part time staff in work you could do**, and/or to cover holiday, sickness, maternity absence. Telephone them to suggest that you could provide these services as a self employed person, thus saving them tax and the hassle of employing people. Providing you also work for one other firm, you are deemed to be self employed and not treated as an employee.

REALLY PRACTICAL TIP Target firms who work in areas you have experience of so that they don't have to spend the first week explaining how their business works, their culture. You can hit the ground running and be available for all the staff holidays, maternity leave. If you need to work from home you could operate as a Virtual P.A.

- **Harness the expertise, experience you have gained over a number of years in employment**. Sit down and make a list of all the people who you have had dealings with in the past few years and then plan to visit them.

If the person you knew has moved on find out where they have gone, as well as getting to know the present incumbent, this way you have two 'bites at the cherry'.

REALLY PRACTICAL TIP By starting your research with people you know, you can practise your research techniques before having to go 'in cold' with people who have never met you.

Ring up past contacts and say you are now freelance, and would like to come and talk about what's going on in their part of the world – you may have to use a letter or e-mail to secure an interview.

- **People providing Alternative/Complementary Therapies** should talk to the local Department of Health to see if they can provide a list of GP's who are known to be empathetic to these types of therapies. By visiting them you may be able to ask them to signpost clients, or display your literature in the Waiting Room.

In most parts of the country there are Centres/Clinics where alternative therapy practitioners see patients. By hiring a room to see a patient, you may then get permission to display your leaflets, be able to attend meetings and give talks and generally network. To carry out your face-to-face questionnaires you might talk to people coming out of health food shops or such clinics.

- **Planning to set up a restaurant or café** it is important to gather information about all the other places people can eat – your competitors. Get hold of their menus, go and have some refreshments, note the number of people they can seat at any one time, note the occupancy rates for different times of the day, days of the week – are they only full on certain nights? Note the attitude of the staff and the general service levels.

Make a note of every single item that you will have to provide in the way of fixtures and fittings, e.g. tables, chairs, china, cutlery, table ware, floor covering, lighting, counters, display areas, tills, menus, pictures, sign writing, cooking/storage equipment. You also need to carry out some face to face interviews using market research questionnaires.

- **If you create things that you hope to sell – jewellery, paintings, greetings cards, pottery, sculpture and other art and craft work**, it is important to talk to people who sell these items. Visit gallery owners, shops who stock these items, craft fairs and exhibitions, to show them your portfolio of work and to get their views on what makes them decide to stock the different types of creations and what is currently selling. They, after all, are likely to have their finger on the pulse of what type of artistic creation will sell.

It is important to carry out this research before you spend a lot of time creating things you think are wonderful, because you may find yourself in a minority - **unlike most other things that are sold, people don't know what they want until they see a new creation!**

A lady I knew was introduced to the art of decorating goose eggs in her early seventies which re-awakened a love of painting she had as a girl. She was offered a table once a month at a local Craft Fair. At first she painted and decorated the eggs in a way that she liked, and sold only one or two. People asked her if she would paint and decorate eggs for them with personalised messages and with jewels and other glitzy adornments. Whilst these requests were not to her taste she concentrated on creating what people had requested and her eggs started selling like 'hot cakes'.

Market Research – Costs

It is very important to gather, as part of your research, as many facts as you can **about what everything is going to cost – to acquire assets, to start up and to operate.** Every bit of information you will need is out in the public domain. You need to understand the significance and difference between **fixed costs** and **variable costs.**

Acquiring Assets – Capital Costs

You may need to buy equipment/furniture/a vehicle to help you provide your product or service. These are assets which wear out (depreciate) over a period of time and will need replacing or updating. You will need to find out what it will cost you to acquire these assets (whether new or second hand). You should find out what the repayments will be if you decide to acquire them on H.P. terms or by renting/leasing them, as an alternative to initially purchasing the items, to conserve your capital.

You should get valued any assets you already own, such as your domestic car and your computer. Your car can be valued by asking a local garage, or by looking up any of the published Used Car Price guides on sale in newsagents or on the internet. Your computer should be valued on the basis that it will normally be depreciated over three years, therefore after the first year it will be worth two thirds of what you paid for it, and so on.

You will need to have an understanding of the differing methods of acquisition to see which items you buy attract capital allowances. You can claim the full costs of leasing equipment/assets in the year you spend the money, but the assets are not yours. Consult an Accountant (see Chapter 2 - Planning Your Business - How to find an Accountant) to see which method is most tax efficient or best use of your capital.

Start Up Costs

You will have to spend money on a number of items before you actually start to generate income, such as stock/materials, insurances, advertising, stationery, printed literature, licences, rent in advance, professional advice, cost of telephone calls/use of the internet, travel costs including use of your domestic car. **There is a formula you can use to establish the 'pence per mile' cost of running your car – see formula in this chapter.**

> **REALLY PRACTICAL TIP Keep receipts for everything you spend up to a year, prior to your start date. These costs can then be set against the income in your first period of trading. You may want to reimburse your personal account from the income from your business as funds permit.**

Operating Costs

You will need to establish from your research how much it will cost to operate your business. You should make a list of all the things you will spend money on, including those items you spent money on before you started but which will continue to form part of your expenditure. Refer to the list of items on the Profit and Loss forms, provided with your Business Plan (from your Bank), or later in this book. (See Chapter 10 - Typical Items of Capital, Revenue and Working Capital Expenditure – Financial Planning and Items which may be claimed in Chapter 12 – Taxation.)

Charging for your Time / Labour

Another important aspect is to work out **how much to charge for your time/labour,** and if you employ someone their cost (try the Job Centre, newspapers, job adverts, trade associations for rates of pay).

As regards **charging for your time**, start by establishing what you would be paid to be employed doing what you do. You need to add to this rate a premium (of say 40%) to reward you for all the other roles you will have as Managing Director, Marketing Manager, Accounts/ Sales Manager and Tea Boy/Girl.

Where you have years of experience/expertise you can consider charging a further premium, for giving your clients a 'fast track' to being able to make increased profits or savings in costs. They will benefit from that experience without having you on the payroll, so you want some of that increased profit/savings in costs – say 10% of the first year's results. Build that into your fee, by charging multiples of your daily rate to reflect the sharing of the benefit.

Don't tell them of your method, but don't feel guilty in charging them what may seem excessive compared with what you used to earn when employed!

> **REALLY PRACTICAL TIP Just 'roll the pitch' about what increased profits, or savings in costs they will achieve as a result of your advice, consultancy/help before you break the news to them about your fee.**

Work out **how much stock/material** you need to hold and how much credit you will need to carry, and the cost of doing so. This can be derived from your sales estimates, whether and how much can be sold for cash/credit and how long you need to hold stock/ materials to produce or provide a service.

It is vital to make this list. Find out (do not guess) what everything will cost, to establish the total amount of money you need to start up, acquire assets and operate your business.

You need to do this before you begin spending significant amounts of money, because you may find the total comes to rather more than you expected. This may put a different complexion on the viability of your venture.

Fixed Costs

Fixed costs, also known as indirect costs and best known as overheads, are those you incur whether or not you sell anything, e.g. rent, insurances, depreciation, utilities, payroll.

The amounts of some of these costs may be 'variable' e.g. how much power you use in producing your products, if you have to pay your staff for overtime occasionally, but for accounting purposes are treated as 'overheads' (fixed costs).

Variable Costs

These are costs you incur as a result of making sales. They will typically be stocks/materials, cost of sales staff, costs of production. They are also known as 'direct' costs.

You need to know which is which when considering your pricing. (See Chapter 4 - Marketing, and Chapter 10 - Financial Planning - your Profit and Loss Account.)

Survival Budget

Another very important reason for establishing your costs, your estimated sales and your profit is to check that your business can provide you with sufficient money to meet your monthly domestic outgoings – you will need a Survival Budget.

Business Plan formats usually provide you with a template showing a list of all the individual elements of your domestic costs and income to carry out this check.

If at first your net profits from the business do not provide you with sufficient money to cover your monthly domestic outgoings, you will need to do a 'Break Even' calculation (see Chapter 10 - Financial Planning) to establish when you hope to start making sufficient profit. You will need to discuss this with your Business Bank Manager and arrange overdraft cover accordingly.

Formula for Assessing the 'Pence Per Mile' Cost of Running Your Vehicle

You need to establish the following costs of running your vehicle, inclusive of the business use:-

1. **Tax** ££££

2. **Insurance** ££££

3. **Fuel** – you need to establish :-

A   The average 'miles per gallon' you get from your car

B   The pence per litre/£ per gallon you pay – multiply the pence per litre figure by 4.54 to arrive at a £ per gallon rate e.g. £1.00 per litre x 4.54 = £ 4.54 per gallon There are 4.54 litres to the gallon

C   Lastly you need to estimate how many miles you expect to travel in the year, including your business travel

So if you expect to travel 9000 miles a year and your car does 30 miles to the gallon, you will need to buy 300 gallons a year at, say, £4.54 per gallon which equals £1,362 ££££

4   **Servicing** Most cars need servicing at least every 10,000 miles and some only at 20,000 mile intervals ££££

5   **Tyres** ££££

6   **MOT** ££

7   **Depreciation** You need to establish how much your vehicle 'depreciates' in value each year – look up the Used Car Price Guide £££

Total Costs ££££

Let us say, for the purpose of this exercise, that the 'all up' total costs of running your vehicle amount to £3000 per year and you expect to travel 9,000 miles, the 'pence per mile' cost will be 33.3 pence per mile. To do the sum you multiply the '£' figure by 100 to get to the pence figure and then divide by the mileage figure, e.g. 300,000 pence divided by 9,000 miles equals 33.3 pence per mile.

Market Research – Competitors

In starting your business you have got to be better than and different from the other people out there already – your competitors.

Why should anyone use you, someone they have never heard of? It is imperative you find out as much as you can about your competition.

Being cheaper is a course of action I suggest you do not take. You may well get business but once your competitors realise they are losing trade to you they will reduce their prices (they have greater reserves than you). They will put you out of business and then put their prices back up again.

Compile information about your competitors:

- **Who are they?**
- **Where are they?**
- **What are their strengths and weaknesses?**
- **Who is their target market?**
- **At what level of quality do they market themselves?**
- **What are their prices – are you comparing like with like?**
- **How do they promote their business?**

Some of this information is relatively easy to obtain from your Desk Research – telephone directories, the internet, some by observation where premises can be visited, some by local enquiry (reputation) – ask at the local post office, pub, village stores – ask your Business Bank Manager, talk to people at business club meetings, look at their web site and at all the advertising they do. Ring them up, purporting to be a potential customer, and ask for references and details of their service, price lists, sales literature.

Are your competitors targeting the same type of customers as you or some other sector?

Are they top quality, somewhere in the middle, or 'stack it high and sell it cheap' operators? Where are you going to position yourself?

> **REALLY PRACTICAL TIP You might consider approaching people in a similar line of business, but in a neighbouring county who may be prepared to tell you the 'tricks of the trade' – or they may tell you to go away. If you don't ask and all that!**

> **A HUGE REALLY PRACTICAL TIP**
>
> **IF THERE IS NO COMPETITION BE VERY WARY!**

You may indeed be the first person to have thought about setting up such a business in the area, but others may have been that way before, have tried and failed. They may have failed because they were incompetent, or it could just be that there was insufficient trade in that area to sustain such a business.

Produce a matrix on paper showing all your competitors, their strengths and weaknesses and comparing them with yours. (See Chapter 14 – Other Considerations - SWOT Analysis).

Consider how you plan to be better than them!

> **REALLY PRACTICAL TIP One of my favourite philosophies of life is that it is not too difficult to be better than the other people out there in competition with you. If you bother to do that little bit more, if you pay attention to the detail, if you think about things from the other person's point of view, the customer, then you will indeed be better than the others who tend to broad brush their way through life – who do just enough to get by!**

In this country we have all had experiences which left us wondering 'am I a paying customer, or just a nuisance?'

If you go into a restaurant and it's just after 'last orders' time you are sometimes told you are too late, either because the waiting staff don't want to be kept late or the chef has closed the kitchen – a sort of Chef's Rest Home!

How often do you have to wait in for someone to come and fix a machine – how often do they ring to tell you when they are likely to arrive or more likely that they are going to be late?

How often, when you go abroad on holiday, has the travel company failed to provide you with important information, key directions on how to find your holiday accommodation?

How rare it is to find companies like 'Virgin Holidays' and the 'Magic of Italy, Spain' who send you really practical information on, for example, how to find your hire car, how to get out of the airport, which lane/sign to look for to be in the right lane on a multi-lane highway, detailed directions on getting safely to your destination. They have sent someone out there to see what you will see – to take the hassle out of what is usually a pretty stressful experience – getting there. They are thinking of the customer.

I am sure you can think of many examples in your domestic or business life where you wonder how businesses survive because of the poor service.

IT IS NOT SO DIFFICULT TO BE BETTER THAN THE OTHER PEOPLE OUT THERE!

SUMMARY

It is vital to acquire as many facts as you can about every aspect of your proposed business. Don't guess where you can get information. Starting your business on a series of guesses will mean that you are operating on a hope and a prayer, which is a very unsound way to operate and likely to end in failure and debts.

Once you have started you will not have time to find out the facts, so take the time to do so before you start.

From my experience it takes on average five months from the moment you decide to start a business to taking your first money, if you are doing thorough research and preparation.

Results of your Market Research

Once you have gathered the information, you must act on it. You cannot ignore the results just because they do not agree with your original ideas.

You may well have to change your plans to reflect the feed-back you have received, but it is far better to make changes at this early stage, rather than face costly and possibly disastrous consequences later.

Your Business Plan should show solid evidence of the research and sampling which you have carried out, as well as the results obtained and actions you have taken, or plan to take, based on those results.

CHAPTER FOUR

MARKETING

Having gathered as many facts as you can about the areas you need to research – the four 'Cs' you need to convert the information to a Marketing Plan – the 4 'Ps':

- Product/Service

- Price

- Place

- Promotion

Product/Service

Having talked to a number of potential customers you will hopefully have identified a product or service that enough of them said they needed, couldn't obtain, or were dissatisfied with existing suppliers, which you can supply at a profit.

You may feel, therefore, that all you have to do is open up for business, tell everyone you are now open and wait for the business to roll in – wrong!

Even if you have the monopoly on supply, unless you understand what will make people use your service, acquire your product, unless you understand how to 'trigger the buying motive' in all the things you do to 'market' your business, you will not get past 'first base'.

Features/Benefits

So it is vital to understand what makes any of us buy something. Why do we buy it and what are we thinking when we make that decision?

We are attracted in the first place by the **'Features'** of what something is, what it looks/sounds like, but what makes us buy something is what it will do for us, the '**Benefits'.**

What we are saying to ourselves is –

WHAT'S IN IT FOR ME?

- What are the 'Benefits' to me?

These are some of the main 'buying motive'/benefits:

- Time Saving

- Money Saving

- Money Making

- One up on your Neighbours/Competitors

- Peace of Mind

- Satisfaction of a Job Well Done

- Value for Money

- Added Value

- Pleasure

- Quality of Life

- Freedom – by obeying the Law

- Stress free Living

It is important to try and think of a benefit or benefits which make you different from, better than, your competitors – your U.S.P., your Unique Selling Point.

This need not be some fantastic 'new wheel' you have invented, it could be that you have a combination of skills that means customers only need to talk to you, not a number of different providers of the service. It could be you have years of expertise and will give them a quality job you can guarantee. It could just be that being reliable and mature you will be different from the other people providing services in the area e.g. garden maintenance, window cleaning, maybe people who don't always turn up!

The important thing to remember is that in everything you say when you are face to face with customers, in your literature, in your letters/e-mails, your web site, your advertising and promotional material, you need to 'shout from the rooftops' what the 'benefits' are to customers using your product and service. Why you are different from and better than your competitors – to think about the 'benefits' from the customer's point of view.

WHAT'S IN IT FOR THEM – the customer?

I attended a talk given by a leading Marketing guru a few years ago who said that consideration of a business' U.S.P. was the first subject he raised when visiting businesses. He always asked the marketing people to tell him what they thought their U.S.P. was - and they told him. Then he asked them to show him their marketing material. The majority of businesses failed to make any mention of their U.S.P. in any of their marketing material - they assumed potential customers out there would know!!!!!

Before you go and see someone think about what are the **benefits to them of using you**; in this way you will condition your mind into asking them questions to make them think about your 'benefits'.

When you write a letter/e-mail or create some promotional material, read it through to see whether the '**benefits**' leap out of the page/screen.

When you design a web site use the front page to 'yell out' the '**benefits**' – don't put your name in big letters across the top, or a big photograph – use the space to perhaps pose some questions for which you have the answers – the '**benefits**'.

It is vital to understand this principle in 'marketing' your business.

Pricing

Many people starting in business make the fundamental mistake of thinking that they must be the cheapest amongst all their competitors if they are to succeed. Others set their price by adding a percentage to the wholesale price, as advised by their suppliers, which indeed might be the right price at a moment in time. It will not take account of the individual cost elements of the changing market place. Others believe that the money they build into their price in respect of their labour costs/their time, is their profit. If you are only working to cover your labour you might as well be employed. You must make a profit, you are entitled to make a profit. You are the one working all hours, you are the one taking the risk and you need the profits to plough back into your business, to broaden the base, before you can start to reward yourself.

Setting your Pricing Strategy is one of the most important features of your Business Plan, if you are to make a profit.

There are a number of factors you will need to take into account in pricing your product or service:

- **Your costs** - you must be certain that you recover all your costs, including making a contribution to covering your overheads and replacing your vehicle, equipment.

For example, people selling things at a craft fair might feel that the profit on their day's activities is the difference between the amount they took and the cost of the goods they bought.

They also need to consider how much time they spent in buying, making the goods they sold, their time spent travelling to and from the fair, and the hours they spent at the fair (how much is their time worth per hour). Also the cost of the table, and of course they needed to have taken money as a contribution towards replacing their vehicle and computer and covering their other overheads/fixed costs.

- **Your expected sales volume** – at first your sales will be low and so your overheads (fixed costs which are not affected by how much you sell) will have to be spread over fewer sales. The unit cost element will be higher, but as your sales increase, with stable overheads, the unit cost element will decrease.

- **What level of quality do you want to project?** – if you pitch your prices too low potential customers might think you are some sort of 'cowboy' outfit; if you pitch them too high people will automatically expect high quality.

- **The level of Profit likely to be achieved – the Gross Profit Margin 'market norm'** – every business in this country is required to report to Her Majesty's Revenue and Customs on a Tax Return the: (a) Value of Sales they made, (b) the Direct cost of those sales i.e. stocks, materials, sales staff, production, and, (c) all their other costs which are generally termed Overheads/Expenses.

The Gross Profit Margin is arrived at by taking (b) away from (a) and the resultant figure when expressed as a percentage of Total Sales (a) is known as the Gross Profit Margin percentage.

There is an average ('norm') Gross Profit Margin percentage for every sector of the market, which is published by an organisation called 'Croner', which can be accessed by Bank Managers and Accountants. By asking any of these organisations you should be able to establish the average GPM for your sort of business – if your Accountant or Bank Manager has a wide portfolio of businesses, including ones like yours, they should be able to tell you from their experience.

- The **Net Profit Margin** is arrived at (by taking (c) your Fixed Costs/Overheads away from (b minus a) your Gross Profit) and is the amount left, and upon which you will be taxed. This is also the amount from which you can take Drawings (if you are a Sole Trader or Partnership) and reinvest the remainder.

- The **'Market Place' price** – what your competitors charge. It is important to remember that the 'market price' **is the price customers expect to pay,** so why be cheaper than everyone else?

When you first start your business you may find that your overheads are less than your competitors, because you are

probably working from home. You may be tempted, therefore, to start with a lower price to get the business.

You should remember that as your business grows **you may have to move out of your home and incur premises costs and other** costs of taking on additional resources and have to start charging VAT. These should have been built in to your initial pricing as **'notional costs'**, for the day when you would have to incur higher overhead costs. If you fail to look ahead you will find it almost impossible to raise your prices to reflect the higher overheads. These costs will therefore have to be covered by taking a reduction in your labour cost/profit.

> **REALLY PRACTICAL TIP If you start your business charging similar prices to your competitors, but with lower overheads, the higher profits you will make should be put aside and used in due course to fund the expansion of your business.**

- **Your 'USP' – your Unique Selling Point**. (See this Chapter - the 'Features and Benefits' section.) If what you have to offer is different from, better than, the competition then you can charge a higher price. As the word gets around, so hopefully your order book will fill up and people will have to wait longer or be prepared to pay more – it's called Supply and Demand.

You need to capitalise on your USP until your competitors find out what it is that you are doing that makes you better than them. If you have been able to patent your idea, or secure a monopoly lower cost source of supply, then you could benefit for a considerable period of time. Otherwise the competition will try to find out and then match your USP.

- **Pricing Variations** – such as 'loss leaders', lower cost sources of supply/production, discounting, special offers, 'price loading' where customers expect to pay higher prices, seasonality.

Loss Leaders - a strategy practised by supermarkets, where for example, they sell petrol at less than they pay for it (at a loss) to get people to then go on to shop in their stores and buy products on which they make good profits. Not a strategy for start up businesses!

Lower Cost Source of Supply – by using Search Engines on the internet it may be possible to secure a lower cost source of production/supply. Use this benefit to make higher profits, not as an excuse to lower your price.

Discounting, Special Offers - devices used to shift slow moving stock or as an initial offer to generate interest. Sometimes it can be used to secure a large order and to encourage early payment.

Price Loading – on the basis that differing levels of price are charged for the same goods or services in different parts of the country, customers will expect to pay higher prices in areas where the cost of living is higher, or where people are more concerned with quality and an excellent service and where the price is of secondary importance, or perhaps not even mentioned. You are not 'ripping' people off – they just want a really top quality product or service.

Seasonality – this is back to Supply and Demand, where what you sell is only in demand at certain times of the year.

Pricing Formula

Having taken into account some of the above factors in determining your pricing strategy, the main elements of your price should cover:

1. Your **labour costs** (keep a log of your time for specific jobs, include travel time to and from job and the costs of people you employ). See Chapter 3 for how much to charge for your labour.

2. The **Cost of Sales** (e.g. the stocks, materials, cost of production, cost of selling).

3. A **Contribution to Overheads/Fixed Costs** (divide total monthly overheads by number of jobs per month/days operating per month to arrive at a per job or a per day unit rate.

1 + 2 + 3 = Total Costs

4. Add a **Profit Margin** as a percentage of Total Costs

Add 1 + 2 + 3 + 4 then compare with

5. The **'Market Place Price'** for a similar product/service

If you find in doing the calculations that you have a price below the 'Market Place' price, just check that you haven't missed some element of your costs, or built in a big enough profit margin, or 'notional' costs of future increases in overheads.

If you find that your price is above the M.P.P., then just check to see whether you are taking too long to do the job, or whether you are paying too much for your supplies, or that your overheads are too high. Do you really need an office and a smart car to do the business?

Resist the temptation to start your business being the 'cheapest'!

Other Considerations

REALLY PRACTICAL TIP If you keep getting a 'yes' every time you quote, try to ratchet up your price until you start getting no's'. Then you know you have got it about right. If you get rejections ask people why they didn't give you the business, how much were you out?

ANOTHER REALLY PRACTICAL TIP Never quote a price off the top of your head. If you are discussing a job and someone asks you how much you are going to charge, turn it round and say 'what were you expecting to pay? Let me go away and provide you with a quote reflecting your budget, but let me also quote you for what will give you a quality job first time around'. That should shame them in to not settling for their 'cheap' alternative!

**Your best price is the one which covers all your costs, makes
you a profit and which the customer feels is giving them
excellent value/service – its worth to the customer.**

Place/Position

You will need to consider the following in determining the **'place to
be' or the 'position'** to take in the market place:

- Where to locate for the convenience of your customer, if they
  have to come to you. For example, in the case of a retail
  outlet, is it easy for them to park, do enough people walk past
  the shop, are there other shops nearby stocking the other
  sorts of things people might need, are there enough potential
  customers living in the area surrounding your premises?

- Where to locate if you have to travel to your customers in
  terms of the time spent. For example, try to put together a
  portfolio of customers which does not involve spending most
  days travelling to see them.

- Where is it best to advertise? Where do your competitors
  advertise?

- At what level of quality to move into the market? Remembering
  that everything you do or say must project the same level
  of 'quality'. Potential customers will be influenced by the
  outward manifestations of your business even before they
  meet you – your cards, your stationery, your advertising, the
  way the phone is answered, the way you and your vehicle
  look – nothing must let you down from the level of quality you
  are trying to project.

- How will you get your product/service to the customer? What is the most cost effective method of distribution/supply, e.g. retail, mail order/internet, delivery, personal call?

Promoting Your Business

PEOPLE DO NOT BUY FROM PEOPLE THEY DO NOT KNOW EXIST!

It is vital to have a rolling three month promotional plan when you first start, to tell potential customers by various means, that you are now open for business and to communicate the benefits of your product/service. This process needs to continue until the 'word of mouth' recommendations account for a large percentage of new business.

How can you most effectively communicate the 'Benefits' and which media should you use?

You need to trigger the 'buying motive' in the minds of your potential customers in everything you do, say and write. They will be attracted by the **'Features'** but what the decider will be is whether the **'Benefits'** to them of your product or service are better than your competitors – so you need to bring out the 'benefits'. (See this chapter - Features and Benefits.)

There is a proven formula for any advert, direct mail letter, presentation, sales visit, telephone call, web site –

'A.I.D.A.'

Attention - Make an impact with an eye catching headline or an attention grabbing statement.

Interest - Keep them reading or listening – what's in it for them?

Desire - Create a desire to respond by convincing them of the benefits to themselves.

Action - Make it easy for people to buy by using website/ e-mail address, freephone number, a map, postcode for Satnav., if they have to visit your premises.

When deciding on **which media to use** you need to consider the following:

- Who is your target market – which part of the population, or sector of the business market?

- Where are they likely to see the message? It is no good taking an advert in a free newspaper if your potential customers don't read the newspaper.

- What key benefits will persuade them to buy?

- How can they get them?

- Where do your competitors advertise?

- Which medium will be most cost effective?

Consider using some of the following media:

- **Business Cards/Letterheads** – invest in good quality graphic design, good material. Don't settle for cheap deals as it will give the impression you settle for second best! Make sure that the font style and logo and 'Pantone' Ink colour are consistent in all of your printed material.

- **Leaflets** – a leaflet is an economical way to tell people you exist. It should say on the front what you have to offer in the headline – don't put your name at the top – they aren't buying your name. Put that at the back of the leaflet together with all the contact details. A leaflet should be something you can read in about a minute. Have a series of bullet points listing the **'Features'** and another listing the **'Benefits'**.

Then tell them how to contact you, find you (a map). Think about the design of your leaflet if you are likely to have them on display. Will the key information on the front be obscured by adjoining/overlapping leaflets?

> **REALLY PRACTICAL TIP** Don't hand out your leaflets to everyone – use them like a snipers bullet, not buckshot! Which hands do I need to put them into, whose offices, which houses have people that are likely to buy? Don't just scatter them to all and sundry.

- **A brochure** can be expensive to produce and is not really necessary at the start up stage.

Some people I have seen over the years had spent a great deal of time producing a brochure before doing any market research. This was a means of being seen to be doing something, but was really an excuse not to go out and talk to people. They hoped that by sending out their brochure work would just flood in.

Using a Web site as your catalogue or to show what you have to offer might be a more economical alternative, particularly where you refer to your web site address in other literature you produce, rather than relying on Search Engine Optimisation.

What is also very important is to try and get letters of commendation from satisfied clients/customers, which could be reproduced if a brochure is felt necessary at a later stage, or shown to people as a sales aid.

> **REALLY PRACTICAL TIP** Don't just send out literature as an alternative to getting in front of potential customers. By doing this you are in effect asking it to do the selling job for you – but there is nothing to beat you seeing someone in person.

- **Yellow Pages/Talking Pages** – this is a media to use for businesses whose services are needed intermittently. Look at the page you are likely to be on and ask yourself: 'how am I going to make my box advert stand out. What words will convey not only what I have to offer, but the 'benefits' of using me?' Don't use a lot of space to headline your name – they aren't buying that. Use words which convey you can be trusted – quality, work guaranteed, fully qualified, references provided. Remember to find out the deadline for getting your advert in.

Do not use a free one-line advertisement unless you are the only supplier for miles around. You can get in to the system at any time using **"Talking Pages'**.

- **Local Press - Press Releases** – cultivate the journalist on your local paper or specialist journal. They are always looking for stories. **They will print your story if it has a novelty or human interest angle.**

REALLY PRACTICAL TIP If you write a Press Release always produce it in Double Spacing between paragraphs to allow them to add their words.

Also remember, if they have space for only so many words and your release is too long they will just take out paragraphs, starting from the bottom, until they have the requisite number of words. If your key messages are somewhere near the end they will get lost in the editing.

If you want all the different media to release the story at the same time, put an Embargo, 'not to be released until a certain time on a certain day', taking into account when different publications hit the system.

You may be telephoned by the advertising department of the paper to take an advert. Ask them if they can couple it with your press release to give **'Advertorial'** You pay for a smaller advert, and get the words in the article, alongside your advert for free!

- **Direct Mail Shots** – use a letter/ e-mail to get in touch with people who were happy to give you their names, addresses and telephone numbers during your market research. Let them know you have started and perhaps offering a discount on their first purchase or an invitation to a grand opening event. Consider using **newsletters, 'Social Networking ' media** to send to your growing list of customers telling them about your latest range, new technological developments.

- **Flyers** – remember, in designing your own flyers, what your reaction is to other peoples' 'bits of paper' coming through your letterbox. Use the 'A.I.D.A.' method to show an 'Attention Grabbing' Headline – **Pose some questions (Features), for which you have the solutions/answers (the Benefits)**. Then tell them how to contact/find you, or that you will call. Use words to convince them that you are 'Bona Fide' – Experienced, Reliable, References Provided, Fully Qualified, etc. Then think about who to give them to, or which houses, which areas, will be reaching your potential customers. It is no good putting your flyers through letter boxes or handing them to people who couldn't afford your service or product.

- **Trade Exhibitions** – at first you probably will not be able to afford to take a stand at a Trade Exhibition and produce the display material. It can be very expensive. Instead, go along to Trade Exhibitions where you will meet potential customers on stands, in the bars, cafés. You will see the latest developments in your field and some of your competitors.

You can claim all the cost of travel to and from the event, entrance fees and refreshments, hotel accommodation, against your business, but not any entertaining you do with people you meet there. Take a good supply of business cards. Collect other peoples' cards and always follow up any contacts you made.

- **Business Club Meetings/Networking** – this can be particularly effective for businesses who sell to other businesses.

Contact your local Chamber of Commerce for details of their forthcoming events, look up **internet 'business networking – your County'** to see other organisations e.g. Federation of Small

Businesses (www.fsb.org.uk), Forum of Private Business (www.fpb. co.uk) Enterprise Agencies (www.nationalenterprisenetwork.org).

Talk to your Bank Manager or Accountant – they may know of other networks.

Remember, going along to meetings (ask if you can come along to one to see what it's like before joining), you will be treated as a fellow human being. They will not know that you are new in business unless you tell them.

You will hear someone speak and when they have finished, discuss with your neighbours what they thought of the content of the talk; you can ask them what sort of business they are in, and hopefully they will ask you what sort of business you are in – if they don't, tell them!

> **REALLY PRACTICAL TIP Don't just give them your card, get their business card and follow up your meeting by telephoning them. Say how glad you were to meet them earlier and that you would welcome an opportunity to go along to explore areas of mutual interest to your businesses, or offer to do a free audit of their part of the operation, which is your speciality. This is likely to be far more effective than looking up potential customers in a Trade Directory and then telephoning them cold to get an appointment.**

At some business club meetings you will be invited to make a one or two minute presentation about your business – **it's called an 'elevator pitch'.**

Don't just tell them what you do but what the 'Benefits' are of using your product or service and then give them your card, and again get theirs to follow up. (See Chapter 14 - for further information on **Networking**.)

- **Giving Talks/Writing Articles -** in going along to Business Club meetings offer to give a talk to a future meeting, if you feel confident about public speaking. Think about who your audience are and their likely areas of interest/needs. Prepare a talk and a Power Point presentation and practise it.

Thank the host for the opportunity to talk. Ask for questions at the end – and always stay for the refreshments afterwards.

People are unlikely to put up their hand sitting in an audience to talk about their particular problem, but they will come up to you afterwards and ask questions. Give them your card and get theirs.

Offer to write an article in the Business Club journal, making sure that they attribute it to you, giving your name and contact details.

- • **Web sites** – the first question to ask is 'do I really need a web site?' To have a really effective site will cost you a lot of money – do you really need it at first? If the answer is 'yes' then ask your Local Enterprise Agency (www. nationalenterprisenetwork.org), Chamber of Commerce (www.britishchambers.org.uk) for a list of web site designers. You may have relatives or friends who know how.

REALLY PRACTICAL TIP Compare them all by asking to see samples of some of their websites. Ask them to tell you the 'hit rates' and the 'sales to hit ratio' for sites where they sell something. Lastly, ask them if they understand the principles of 'marketing'. If they don't, you will probably end up with having a technically excellent site which will sell nothing.

If you use a friend or relative and they turn out not to be very good you will have difficulty 'sacking' them!

Again, use the **'A.I.D.A.'** mnemonic to check whether your website meets these criteria. Don't use the first page with your name in big letters and a large photograph. **Pose a few questions enabling you to spell out the main 'Features' and 'Benefits' of using your product or service.** Tell them who you are and where you are in later screens. Make it easy for them to order and pay, avoiding ambiguity.

If you want customers to find your website amongst the huge number of others you will need to use a designer who understands and can demonstrate how to optimise Search Engine use. This will be expensive.

If you want a site to act as a brochure or catalogue at a reasonable cost you will need to refer to the 'domain name' in your printed literature or adverts. Sometimes you can ask to link in to other 'well known' sites for a fee.

- **Online Social Networking** - Increasingly business owners are using **'LinkedIn', 'Facebook' and 'Twitter' as Promotional marketing tools.**

Ask your Local Enterprise Agency, Chamber of Commerce if they can recommend the names of businesses, clients who specialise in using these marketing tools. Ask around at 'Business Networking' meetings to find the local experts.

CHAPTER FIVE

SELLING

Many people have told me over the years that one of the things that worried them, before starting a business, was that they didn't know how to sell.

They were usually the people on the courses I ran who then took every opportunity during the course to remind us about their product or service (and handed out their business cards at the end – 'let's keep in touch'!). Others had brought in samples of their work to look at over lunchtime – just when everyone else was there eating!

One guy spent the evening of the first day of a three day course preparing individual dishes of his exotic food for us all to have at lunch the next day – he just happened to bring in his menus with his contact details!

You may feel that you do not know how to sell, but we all do, we do it instinctively in our everyday lives in our relationships with other people. We don't call it 'selling' but it is.

- **We sell ourselves to others we meet** – most people like to feel that other people like them and are influenced by the way we 'sell' ourselves.

- Have you ever met anyone who went out of their way to make sure you didn't like them?

- **We negotiate with other adults** – we try to achieve a win-win situation where two parties are seeking different objectives.

- How often do you want to do something which your other half does not want to do and end up with a compromise?

- **We persuade** – getting our small children to eat up their meals!

We therefore can harness our natural skills when 'selling' in the context of operating the business, and we have to start with understanding.

- **What makes each of us want to buy something?**

- **What are our motives?**

When we buy something we are sub-consciously saying to ourselves:

What's In It For Me?

What are the Benefits to me?

By understanding ourselves, our motives, we should be able to persuade other people to buy. We should be able to sell by asking them questions, making them think about the 'Benefits'.

What's In IT For Them?

What are the benefits to them of our product/service? (See Chapter 4 - Marketing - Features and Benefits.)

Selling 'face to face' is about having a conversation with someone by asking a series of 'open' questions to find out information, their problems, their needs and then matching the 'features and benefits' of your product/service to their needs.

Selling is not telling people about how wonderful your product or service is, and hoping they will buy.

A young guy came on one of my training courses who had discovered a device for attaching to shower heads (made in the U.S.A.), which reduced the use of water by 25% and the heating costs of the water also by 25%. He told us that it was a big seller in the U.S., but he had not had much success selling it over here. He had been going around hotels, gyms and swimming pools asking people if they would like a demonstration. Most people said they were too busy. I suggested he stopped using that tactic, but to ring up, find out the name of the decision maker, go and see them by appointment and ask just two questions. 'How much money do you spend at this hotel, gym etc each year, using and heating water?' They will give you two figures. Then ask them if they would like a demonstration of the device which will save them 25% of their annual water usage and their heating costs, quoting the actual amount of money saved. I saw him later, and he told me it had transformed his success rate.

Properly handled, and by making someone think about other aspects (perhaps taking them out of their 'comfort zone') by highlighting the 'benefits' of your product/service it is possible your potential customers will conclude as to how they managed to get this far without your product/service?

There are five stages to the Selling process (face to face), and there are some 'tricks of the trade'/techniques which will help you to be successful:

1. **Preparation**

2. **Opening the Sale**

3. **Identifying the Customer Needs - Matching with your Benefits**

4. **Recognising the Buying Signals**

5. **Closing the Sale**

Stage 1 - Preparation

Compile as much information as you can about the people you are hoping to sell to before you go and see them. Be totally focussed on THEM.

As regards **members of the public** try to pick up clues by taking into account what they are wearing, their car and/or if you visit them at their homes take in all the manifestations of their life-style – the way the garden looks, what things they have in the house, photographs of children, grandchildren, ornaments and so forth – see if you can establish things of mutual interest from what you are observing.

If you are going to see **people in business** who are Companies then look them up in **Kompass** or **Key British Enterprises**. If they are not Companies then arrive 15 minutes early for the appointment and look around at what is on display in the waiting room, press cuttings, 'Mission Statements' on the wall, talk to the secretary/ receptionist to find out as much as you can about the individual you are about to see and the firm.

Know your own limitations – if you are asked if you could handle a large order and you couldn't, don't waffle!

Know as much as you can about your competitors – some people you go to see will claim that your competitors can do such and such a thing (as a try-on) and they will soon know whether you have done your homework.

By doing all this preparation you are signalling to people that you have bothered, you are a thorough operator and consider them important. Go armed with supplies of business cards and look tidily dressed.

Long ago, when I was a newly employed oil company sales rep., I called on a competitor's garage without an appointment hoping to persuade them to change their petrol supplier (as part of a national campaign). I had previously seen them quite often without appointments and they had bought some lubricants. The day I arrived the boss wasn't available. I waited. When he did arrive there was a 'panic' job which he had to see to. I waited. Then he went for lunch and said he was too busy. I made telephone appointments for all my other calls for that campaign and from then on sat down each week to decide what I was going to try and achieve on each of my visits to the same garages I called on regularly. It was no good going in saying 'don't your petrol pumps look smart' and passing the time of day with the owners !!!

Stage 2 - Opening the Sale

When you telephone or visit someone they will be in the middle of doing something else or have other things on their mind. You will be seen as a nuisance and it's going to cost them money or time. They are going to have to stop doing what they want to do and listen to you. So you have to convince them that your service/product is an investment and that you are genuinely interested in providing them with solutions to their problems, meeting their needs. They may also not remember why you are there.

So once in front of them, open with a positive statement of what you have come to talk about, demonstrate that you have done your homework, are properly prepared and refer to your letter/e-mail sent in advance, and if possible to some press report or other external manifestation of the benefits of your product or service.

Stage 3 - Identifying/Meeting Customer Needs

At a later stage in my oil company career I was responsible for setting up some new lubricant distribution centres in London, Birmingham, Manchester and Glasgow I invited all the main equipment suppliers to come in to discuss their products, vehicles, fork lift trucks, storage racking, and so forth. The fork lift sales reps. who came to see me all assumed that, as we were a big oil company we must need their most expensive, computer controlled, all singing and dancing equipment. The one company who asked me to describe how our warehouse storage, order picking, vehicle loading and delivery operation would work, got the contract.

Selling is not about 'telling' people what you have – here is my product buy, buy, buy! **It is about asking questions to identify their likely needs.**

Questions which you should have asked when you went in initially in 'market research' mode.

Get people talking about themselves and their business.

Ask **'open'** questions – what, where, when, why and how – make notes of their answers. Lead them by your questioning into lateral thinking about other aspects, other ways of doing something, which ideally can be satisfied with the benefits of your product or service.

Will it:-

- **Save them time?**

- **Save them money?**

- **Make them more money?**

- **Give them an advantage over their neighbours/competitors?**

- **Give them pleasure?**

- **Give them a better quality of life?**

- **Give them peace of mind?**

- **Give them a benefit?**

Stage 4 - Recognising the Buying Signals

There will come a stage in your questioning when the person you are talking to will be signalling to you, by their 'body language' that they want to buy, you have convinced them. They will be leaning forward, smiling, agreeing, asking clarifying questions, perhaps picking up your literature to have another look.

When you see these signals, whatever you do, stop asking questions, 'zip up' and use one of the 'Closing the Sale' techniques.

Do not go on asking about other things – their interest will go cold and you will lose the sale. Catch them later with those. **Strike while they are really interested!**

Stage 5 - Closing the Sale Techniques

In this country we play a little game when it comes to Closing a Sale – I like to think of it as 'Serious Fun'.

In America, in the movies, they always seem to use the 'Direct Close' – 'O.K. Buddy can I have the Order?'

There are different ways of Closing the Sale:

1. **The Alternative Close** – Where you are pretty certain by their body language that **they do want to buy** offer to quote for either a Pilot Exercise or the Whole Contract. Ask them to choose between alternatives: Would you like to pay by cash or credit card? Would you like this one or that one? Either way you get part or all of the order/contract.

2. **The Summary Close** – Again, where you are sure from the buying signals, stop asking questions and recap on all the points

which were discussed, highlighting their needs and confirming how you would satisfy them. Follow this up with:

3. **The Direct Close** – Ask for the Order. Ask if you can quote/ tender.

4. **The Concession Close** – Sometimes you may feel that the only way you are going to get an order is to offer a little extra, special terms. But only where there has been an objection, which you feel can only be satisfied with a concession. Keep such offers close to your chest until you feel there is no other option.

5. **'Keep the Door Open' Close** – Use this technique where clearly the person you are talking to needs more time to consider, or has another appointment waiting. Make another date to come back to see them. Send them a letter or e-mail confirming the main points of your meeting and the next date. This serves as the start point for your next meeting. They will switch off and forget what you said as soon as you leave!

Overcoming Objections – If objections are raised do not answer them with a glib answer (you will risk making them look stupid!). Pause, make a note of the objection and ask if you can come back to it. Give them the impression that they have got you by your reaction. This will give you time to think of what you are going to do about it, or by further questioning they usually realise they have 'jumped the gun' and overcome their own objection. But you didn't make them look stupid!

Use the 'F.E.A.R.' technique – **Again this technique is part of the game:**

- **F**ind out the real reason for the objection
- **E**mpathise – 'that's a good point you raise'
- **A**nswer – by showing how you will deal with their point
- **R**econcile – by ensuring there are no remaining vestiges of concern

After Sales Service/Customer Care

It can take months to get a customer, but it can take minutes to lose one. Customer Care is about following up the sale to make sure they are happy with what you provided.

REALLY PRACTICAL TIP If other people/staff are involved in implementing the 'solution' process, make sure they understand their part by talking to them, not just their manager or the 'boss'. They will 'influence' the decision to buy again from you.

ANOTHER REALLY PRACTICAL TIP Keep talking to your customers about their changing needs, to establish what else you might do for them.

Satisfied customers will come back for more and they will tell others. They will be loyal to your business.

Whilst most businesses involve selling 'face to face', **there will be additional techniques you will need if for example you are running a shop.** In addition to the principles involved in ' face to face' selling, **understanding how to effectively merchandise your products will ensure that customers leave your shop with more than they came in to buy!**. There are training courses to provide you with these additional skills.

CHAPTER SIX

OPERATIONAL ASPECTS – PREMISES and EQUIPMENT

To operate your business you must have somewhere to work and some resources, equipment, transport, tools.

Premises

Working from Home

Most people starting a business do so by using a room or space in their house. It has some advantages and some disadvantages, depending on the circumstances.

Advantages:

- By using your own space you are not having to pay someone else for use of a room or premises. You are not taking on a lease. It is **cost efficient.**

- You **save time** by not having to commute to an office, shop, etc., time you can use to better run your business.

- By working at home, **you reduce the chances of being burgled,** unless your business necessitates people visiting your house (e.g. for holistic therapy, hairdressing).

- You can c**laim on your tax return for the heating and lighting costs of using a room in your house.** Check with your Accountant the amount allowed by the local Tax Office. Don't charge your business rent for the use of a room.

- If you have **family members living in the house they can help you run your business,** by answering the telephone, by stuffing envelopes for a mail shot, delivering leaflets, secretarial or/other work. **You can even pay them up to the annual Personal Allowance limit,** without having to deduct tax and NI Contributions, providing they have no other form of income. This includes, for example, teenage children, who must be capable of doing the work, and the amount you pay them must be reasonable. These costs can be deducted from your income in arriving at the net profit on which you will be taxed, but at a lower level having deducted family members' pay.

- As you are not tied to when someone else's premises are open, **you can start and finish work at home when it suits you.** It is important, however, not to let your business invade your private life. Determine to start and finish at a certain time and then close the office door and put on the answer phone.

Disadvantages:

- If there are **other people in the house they can interrupt/ disturb your work.** It is important to have a set of rules with them, that they must not come in unless it is a matter of life or death – you need a clear run at work tasks and thinking time. They couldn't interrupt if your office was elsewhere.

- It is tempting to be **distracted by other things going on in the house** – sports matches on television, assistance with household chores, children and pets.

- **Do tell your neighbours what you are doing** otherwise they may invent what they think you are doing and if it is causing them a problem could make difficulties – for example by complaining to the Local Authority, causing you to have to move elsewhere and the need to reprint all your stationery and sales literature.

If your business is successful and this begins to show in your lifestyle, envy could affect what had been a stable relationship with your neighbour. Tell them at the start what you are hoping to achieve and the long hours you will have to work to get the better things in life!

I had a guy who came on one of my courses who had discovered that by putting new bodies on old models of a certain '4 x 4' chassis manufactured before a certain year, he could legally avoid paying some taxes in some European countries. I suggested that as he was likely to have a number of these vehicles parked outside his house from time to time that he had better tell his neighbours what he was doing, otherwise they might assume he was involved in some questionable activity and tell the police.

- You may find it **difficult to motivate yourself,** when things are not going so well and there is no one in the office to 'gee' you up on your 'down' days, no-one to say 'come on, come and have a cup of coffee.'

Some Enterprise Agencies offer a facility for a Business Counsellor/ Adviser/Mentor to visit business owners at their own premises. It is good to have someone to talk to, a sympathetic, impartial listener experienced in business.

- Working from home may not project the right **professional image** for your business. Your address may sound like a 'cottage industry' type venture.

> **REALLY PRACTICAL TIP Try inserting 'Suite 1 or Unit 1', in front of your normal postal address; you don't need permission, just explain to your regular postman/woman what is going on. However if you seek any form of credit you will need to officially inform the Post Office.**

- **Answering the telephone** with music playing, babies crying, or dogs barking in the background will take the edge off your attempts to convince the caller that they are dealing with a professional business.

- **You may find it lonely at home** – you will miss the 'camaraderie' of working with other people. It is important to join your local Chamber of Commerce or other business clubs and go along to meetings. You will meet other people running businesses, who may have had the same problem you are having and will share with you how they dealt with it. They may also want to do business with you, it's called 'networking'. (See Chapter 4 - Marketing - Networking and Chapter 14 – Other Considerations.)

It is good to get away from the office.

- **Once you take on staff** and you ask them to work in your home, remember they will have to get up in the morning and come to your house as their office; it won't seem like going to work. If there is no one else to talk to, or the shops are too far away to walk to, they may well leave for another job.

If you take on staff working from their homes, then again you will find managing people from a distance has its difficulties. Try to meet and communicate with them regularly.

- If, for example, you decide to build an **extension to your home to house your expanding business you may well be faced with Capital Gains Tax on that part of your house. Try to have something in the extension to show it is used for domestic purposes as well.**

Other Considerations on Use of Your Home

- **Generally speaking you do not have to inform your Local Authority that you are running a business from home**, unless it is likely to cause a nuisance to your neighbours. For example inconsiderate parking by clients, large vehicles delivering supplies blocking other people's access, or that your business affects the local environment with noise, cooking vapours. Check if in doubt, before having your literature printed.

- **Your mortgage agreement/rental agreement may contain a clause that says you may not conduct a business from home**. This was put in some years ago to stop people from carrying out car servicing, bodywork repairs on residential roads and streets. If your business is office based and you are not doing anything to increase the risk to the property, your mortgage company/landlord are unlikely to stop you, but just check if you have any doubts.

- **You must however inform your Insurance companies that you are making dual domestic/business use of a room in your house, your computer, telephone and other equipment and your vehicle.** Describe what you are doing to show, if appropriate, that there is no increase in risk, no excuse for an increased premium.

> **REALLY PRACTICAL TIP Get a letter from them acknowledging notification of this information, should they say at a later date that they never had your letter when you make a claim!**

Serviced Office Accommodation

Working from home may not be practicable or suitable. Taking on and kitting out your own office is expensive. There is an alternative – **using Serviced Office Accommodation.** In most towns and cities you can hire fully serviced office facilities, by the hour, by the day, and/or a range of services, which you pay for as you use them. They can answer your telephones as if they were your receptionist, get page messages to you, 'hot desking' – using a desk from which to operate your laptop / mobile, you can hire rooms/equipment, make use of secretarial services, or you can use them as a correspondence address.

Details can be found in Yellow Pages or a web site (under 'Serviced Office Accommodation').

Taking on Premises

If you need premises on a fairly regular basis, you may need to consider renting/leasing. Most Local Authorities have regular Property Availability bulletins of both private and public sector premises for rent, to save you trawling round all the local Commercial Estate Agents. If you find a property you like, get hold of the details from the Estate Agent, and get the lease from the Landlord.

Check with the Local Authority Planning office that you can use the premises for your intended purpose.

Have a solicitor look at the lease, who should challenge clauses which require you to fully repair the premises when you leave. He/

she should tell you what your rights are regarding the Landlord and Tenant Act 1954, particularly in respect of whether you have an automatic right to renew the lease if you want to stay on. Short term leases tend not to have this protection.

The Landlord can make you put back the premises to the way you found them, at your cost.

REALLY PRACTICAL TIP Get internal photographs of what it looked like on day one, have a survey done if you are occupying other than just one room in a building. You may find that any item of equipment you fixed to a wall or floor becomes the property of the Landlord.

Negotiate to vary in your favour the terms you are being offered. Ask for a 'rolling break clause' where you are uncertain as to how well you might do - flexibility is important. Use the information from the Property Bulletin to establish the level of other rents terms for similar accommodation.

REALLY PRACTICAL TIP Never enter into an informal arrangement with a friend who tells you it is all right to use part of the space they are renting, without checking that they have the right to sublet. The landlord might turn up one day and send you packing!

For more information see Chapter 8 - Legal Aspects - Premises.

Resources/Equipment

In addition to yourself and your skills/ability/knowledge you will need various assets to enable you to run your business and to help you earn money.

Furniture

You will need a desk, a chair, and **a large filing cabinet** in a separate area in your home or elsewhere to handle all your administration/ paperwork. Do not run this from the end of your kitchen or dining room table.

These items can be obtained by looking up the internet, adverts in the local newspaper, by checking Yellow Pages to see if there are suppliers dealing in second hand furniture/equipment. Some Commercial Estate Agents hold auctions each month.

REALLY PRACTICAL TIP Check with the local Office Furniture shop to see if any local businesses are buying new equipment and may be glad to let you have their old equipment, furniture. Also look for firms which may be closing down.

Communications

Establish what is the minimum amount of telephone equipment you need to run your business. Do you really need multiple lines, telephones, the latest mobiles 'I -phone', answering machines and a computer on internet? All of these bring 'overheads', e.g. line rentals, which all mount up.

Correspondence

If your address is not suitable for business use, you can rent a PO Box at the local post office.

You may want to use a reply paid envelope if you want people to reply to you. You will need a licence from the post office for this.

Computers

Before buying or replacing your computer, consider carefully what you will use this equipment for:

- e–mailing
- social networking

- word processing

- database – to keep a record of clients and suppliers

- spreadsheets – for preparing cash flow and profit and loss forecasts

- accounting – keeping books/financial records, issuing invoices

- presentations – can you use Microsoft Power Point?

- DTP/graphics – to produce better quality documents

Seek up to date advice from shops which sell I.T. equipment, on specifications and on the deals available, and look at publications. Also talk to friends and acquaintances who know about computers to cross reference the information you are given by the shops.

'Microsoft Office' is considered to be one of the **best software packages** for businesses. There are various ways you can buy these, including special deals for students.

Other Equipment

Every business/organisation needs **to make a copy of a document** at some stage. For occasional copies a printer/scanner attached to your computer will also give you 'one off' copies.

The **printer determines the quality** of presentation of the finished work. If this is important, invest in a good quality printer. Also consider whether you want a facility for printing on both sides of the paper.

As your business grows there may be a number of computer users which could benefit from being networked into a common printer.

If you need to produce a large number of multi-page documents you may need to invest in a larger photocopying machine.

> **REALLY PRACTICAL TIP When buying always check the small print on the sales document, particularly regarding maintenance, and if leasing the termination clauses, and always read the back of delivery notes.**

Stationery

You will probably need

- letterheads
- continuation sheets
- compliment slips
- business cards

You may also need

- invoices
- receipt books
- order forms
- rubber stamps
- stickers

Invest in as good quality graphic design and good quality paper as you can afford. You can of course use 'Clip Art' from your computer, but will it look as good as that done by a professional Graphic Designer?

REALLY PRACTICAL TIP Use the back of your business card to list the various products/ services you have to offer and the 'benefits' of using you.

Vehicles

It is likely that using your domestic vehicle for business will be the best option, rather than having one owned by your company/firm. The tax on company car 'benefits' are punitive.

- It is important to get your vehicle valued – you can pick up 'Used Car Price Guides' in newsagents and on the internet, or ask at a garage.

Keep a log either in your diary or a small book you keep in the car, of the miles run in connection with the business. Take a milometer reading when you start your business and then every month. This way you can establish what percentage of your total miles is run on business. You can then claim against the business that percentage of all the costs of running your vehicle, including the initial (business use) value of your vehicle as the start point for subsequent depreciation each year, as a legitimate cost to set against your income to reduce your tax liability. (See Chapter 12 - Taxation - Items which may be Claimed.)

Keep all your fuel receipts, not just to the value of the business miles run. Take copies of receipts for car servicing, repairs and keep receipts for car washes, car parking, etc., where the cost is incurred in the course of your business. Keep these in your business files showing what percentage of the total bill you have set against the business in your 'books'.

- To recover the cost in your charges/prices you will also need to work out what it cost in pence per mile to run your vehicle. (See Chapter 3 - Market Research - Formula for Assessing the Cost of Running your Vehicle.)

Dealing with Suppliers

Shop around before purchasing any equipment and compare prices, delivery and payment terms. Make sure both parties understand what is covered, and if necessary get a written quotation detailing what is included.

Agree Terms and Conditions before you supply a product or service, or when you take delivery of someone else's.

REALLY PRACTICAL TIP If you regularly buy stocks, materials, fuel from a supplier seek to get some benefit from being a regular customer, e.g. discount, extended credit or both. Remember they haven't got to spend money trying to find you as a new customer every so often.

CHAPTER SEVEN

LEGAL ASPECTS

SETTING UP LEGAL STRUCTURES

You have to adopt a **Legal Structure** for your business. The typical structures, each of which has advantages and disadvantages, include:

- **Sole Trader**

- **Partnership**

- **Limited Liability Partnership**

- **Limited Company**

A 'Franchise' is a 'business format' not a structure. You will still need to adopt a legal structure to run a franchise business (see later in this Chapter).

Sole Trader

This is the easiest way of setting up a new business, and usually the most appropriate if you are on your own. You can start immediately, with little capital and no legal formalities.

You need to think of **a name (a Trading Title) for your business** and make sure no one else is already using it (by checking with the Yellow Pages and Companies House (www.yell.com), (www.companieshouse.gov.uk). You also need to check that your logo (a potential trade mark) (www.ipo.gov.uk) and a domain name you plan to use are not already in use with these websites (www.nominet.org.uk) (www.anewbusisness.co.uk). It is just as well to check with

Yellow Pages that no-one has booked to use the name you have chosen in the next issue, before having your stationery printed.

As a Sole Trader you cannot register your name in order to protect it. You could protect the 'style' of your name as a Trade Mark, for example the word 'Virgin' is depicted in red words at an angle. You must not use 'Limited' in your name.

> **REALLY PRACTICAL TIP One way to show that you had the trading title on a certain date is to send yourself an envelope with your trading title, name and address, with a 'certificate of posting' to show that on that date you had that name.**

Unless you trade under your own name (without any addition), you need to show your trading title and your own name and business address on any stationery you use (such as letters, emails, invoices, purchase orders and receipts), together with your name as the 'Proprietor/Owner' in a clearly visible position - the bottom of the page.

You must also have this information on your website and on a notice at your business premises in a prominent position (such as close to your front door) so that your suppliers and customers know the name of the owner and the contact address for official documents and claims. (See Chapter 8 – Business Names.)

You must inform H.M. Revenue and Customs (HMRC) on Form CWF1, within three months of starting to trade. You also need to arrange to pay Class 2 National Insurance contributions. The forms can be downloaded or completed online from their web site (www. hmrc.gov.uk).

Failure to do this could result in you being fined, and if left for a period of time the tax people can come along and invent what they think you have been earning and can tax you on their estimates. They can go back up to six years, so you need to inform them, without fail!

Your business will have to pay Class 4 NI contributions on part of your net profits, which is a sizeable tax. This is included on your tax return and added to the Income Tax you will have to pay.

You must put away every month sufficient funds (e.g. between 20–25% of your net profits) to cover your income tax/Class 4 NI liabilities. This has to be paid to the HMRC by January 31st, following the end of your first trading period (most accountants suggest you draw up your accounts to 31st March each year to tie in with the Tax Year). Thereafter you pay your Income Tax in two equal instalments on July 31st and January 31st. (See Chapter 12 - Taxation).

The money you pay yourself is called 'drawings' – you are in effect 'drawing down' on your net profits to pay yourself. This money is deemed to be part of your net profits and you are taxed on the total 'net profit' figure, not the amount you pay yourself in drawings. You decide on the amount you draw.

To sum up, as a Sole Trader you have complete control and all the profits after tax belong to you. So do all the losses! You do not have to send your accounts to Companies House, for all to see. You are solely and personally responsible for all debts incurred by the business, with no limit to your liability. If the business is unsuccessful or fails because of other peoples'/businesses' actions you could end up owing money, possibly even losing your house.

Partnership

This is where two or more people join forces to run a business. It is important that people going into partnership choose others with complementary skills.

No matter how well you know each other – even if you are related – **a legal agreement is essential.** This applies equally to active or 'sleeping' partners.

This is known as the **'Deed of Partnership'** and should cover at least the following areas:

- What business is included
- Responsibilities and Duties
- Profit Sharing

- Hours of Work

- Limits on Monthly Drawings

- Sickness and Holidays

- Bank cheque signature arrangements

- Duration & Termination

- Capital withdrawals

- Decision making Controls

- Appointing an independent arbitrator where partners can't agree

- Partnership property/partners' personal property

- Removing and recruiting partners

Each partner is 'jointly and severally' liable to third parties for the debts of the partnership, even if incurred through mismanagement or dishonesty by another partner. Ignorance of what your partner was doing is no defence.

It is vital, therefore, that a partnership agreement is drawn up and run past a solicitor once you are all certain you want to go forward with the business. Failure to do this in the event of the partnership not working out, will result in the 1890 Common Law Act being applied. This could drag in all your personal assets if the partnership borrowed a lot of money, or entered into a lease, or ran up a large debt.

I have seen a number of people over the years whose business partners just disappeared one day, leaving them to clear up all the debts. Creditors come after the partner they can find!

All the responsibilities regarding the timing and payment of tax/ National Insurance contributions, are the same as for Sole Traders, mentioned earlier. Each partner is responsible for informing HMRC and paying his or her own tax, as well as completing a Tax return for the partnership. Similarly, the trading title and business address, and the names of all the partners must be shown on any stationery, website and on a notice at the business premises.

Limited Liability Partnership

This is a relatively new legal structure, which can give Partners limited liability, similar to a Limited Company. Unlike partnerships, a LLP is a legal entity in its own right - debts incurred are the LLP's debts and not the personal liability of its members. As a result, LLPs are open to more public scrutiny. They have to file annual returns and accounts.

Traditionally Accountants and Solicitors have been Partnerships, where all partners are 'jointly and severally liable'. With the collapse of the Asian banking conglomerate B.C.C.I. in the early 90's, and latterly with the collapse of Enron in the U.S., some of the larger Accountancy Partnerships have seen their partners lose all their assets. This new structure was introduced to give greater protection for partners in Accountancy and Solicitor practices, but can be used by other types of business.

Members of a LLP could have personal liability, like directors of a company, if they allow the LLP to trade whilst insolvent. LLP members also risk a claw back of profit shares and other benefits received by them in the two years before the LLP's insolvent winding up. In other respects LLPs are similar to partnerships. The members of the LLP are taxed in the same way as partners of a partnership. Also, it is as essential for members of a LLP to have a legal agreement as it is for partners of a partnership. As with partnerships, the trading title and business address, and the names of all LLP members must be shown on any stationery, website and on a notice at the business premises (if in doubt consult a solicitor).

Company limited by shares

A **Limited Company** is a legal entity in its own right. It has its own legal identity and any claims are restricted to the assets of the company. Private Limited Companies are designated as Limited Company after their name (A..B.C. Ltd. Coy).

Public Limited Companies are designated as P.L.C's.

Limited liability means that shareholders have no personal liability assuming the amount payable to the Company on the original allotment and issue of their shares has been fully paid up (i.e. Directors liability is limited to paying back the value of the initial shares). Directors are a little more at risk than shareholders, but only if they are in breach of their duties as directors or if they allow the Company to incur more debt and liabilities with no reasonable prospect of avoiding an insolvent winding up. However, if your own company fails only for reasons your directors could not reasonably have foreseen – e.g. if your major customer failed, causing your own company to fail then the directors should not have personal liability for the debts left outstanding. If as a director you entered into personal guarantees (for a business loan or in signing a lease on behalf of the Company), you must understand that this would take away the limit of your liability to the extent of the guarantee.

To set up a Limited Company you need to get in touch with Companies House (www.companies-house.gov.uk) to request a start up pack. They will require you to **acquire two documents** known as **a 'Memorandum of Association' and 'Articles of Association'**. These can be obtained from a **Company Registration Agent** – an 'off the shelf ' ready made company. **Contact the Association of Company Registration Agents** – (www.acra-uk.org) for a 'bona fide' Agent. The documents can also be custom made to your own specification using an accountant or solicitor Do this if you expect to be a growing complex operation.

> **REALLY PRACTICAL TIP Beware of adverts offering you a company and a bank account for not a lot of money – it's probably a 'scam'.**

Companies House will send you a Certificate of Incorporation and inform your local HMRC office that you are a company. The tax people should send you a form CT 41G to complete – ask for it or download it (www.hmrc.gov.uk), if it doesn't arrive.

> **REALLY PRACTICAL TIP You can set up a Limited Company (to protect your name), but also register and start trading as a Sole Trader. You could consider this where you have a really good name or product, but don't want the bureaucracy of running a company at first.**

You need to inform your local HMRC office of the situation so that you are not sent two tax returns for the two legal entities. You will need to re-register your company every year until you are ready to trade as a limited company. This will normally be at the stage where you are in danger of paying the higher rate of tax on your Sole Trader or Partnership. Income Tax and Corporation tax have differences and you need to get advice from your accountant as to your best course of action to minimise the tax your business pays. (See Chapter 12 - Taxation)

Becoming a Company Director brings with it huge responsibilities which should not be undertaken lightly. Ask your solicitor or accountant what they are. Libraries, Banks, Enterprise Agencies can give you a fact sheet.

It is vital to closely monitor the profit and loss and cash flow situation every month and to take action where it is clear that the company will not be able to meet its 'current liabilities' (outstanding invoices) and 'contingent liabilities' (longer term commitments such as H.P. agreements, leases and statutory liabilities, e.g. redundancy pay). **Professional advice must be sought from an insolvency practitioner as to whether you can continue to trade** and how you should deal with the potential insolvent situation without further risk to the company's creditors and with minimum risk to your directors.

Companies need at least one director who is responsible for ensuring all the legal documentation and Company House administration is complied with. If a company has only one shareholder who is also a director, remember that any contract between the shareholder/director and the company must be recorded in writing and it must be approved by the board at its first meeting after the contract was entered into. Breach of this requirement is an offence. Get advice from a solicitor.

As a Limited Company, the company pays corporation tax nine months and one day after the end of its trading period (this does not have to be exactly 12 months after starting – get advice from your accountant as to the optimum dates for your business). **Again, it is important to put away the tax every month so that it is available when you have to hand it over.**

As a Director of the company, if you have staff **you have to hand over the income tax and NI contributions to HMRC by the 19th of the following month, on salaries/wages.**

Directors can take a combination of salary and dividends to minimise the personal income tax they might have to pay – get advice from your accountant on how best to do this given your set of circumstances.

Franchise

A Franchise is a way of acquiring a proven business idea, where the development work has been done by the 'Franchisor' – the originator of the idea. It is not a guarantee of success, as much depends on how well the 'franchisee' runs the business and also whether the particular product or service is needed in the area of operation.

The 'Franchisor' grants a licence to the 'Franchisee' to operate under the trade name or trade mark of the 'franchisor' and to sell its products and services

There is an initial fee to acquire the 'know how', the systems promotional material, training, materials and/or equipment.

There are further payments either as a management service fee/royalty or a 'mark up' on the cost of products provided by the franchisor.

It is necessary to adopt a legal structure to operate a Franchise, ideally as a Limited Company.

Advantages

- Proven Business Idea Systems
- Initial Training - ongoing advice
- Nationwide advertising / brand
- Possible help from some franchisors with initial funding premises and general support

Disadvantages

- Potentially high initial cash outlay
- Ongoing Management Fee

- You have to stick to their systems
- Not able to readily alter trading methods

Contact the British Franchising Association (www.thebfa.org or tel. no. 01865 379892) to check whether the Franchisor is registered with them. Some Banks offer specialist advice in taking on a Franchise.

Summary of Advantages/ Disadvantages of each Legal Structure

Sole Trader

Advantages

- Total control
- Can start straight away
- Minimum paperwork
- No public disclosure of accounts
- Pay tax well after end of initial trading period
- Lower NI Contributions

Disadvantages

- Unlimited Liability
- Limited access to capital
- No protection of business name
- Death dissolves the business
- Pay higher rate of tax at an earlier stage than a Ltd. Coy
- No DSS unemployment cover if business fails

Partnership

Advantages

- Start straightaway
- Pooling of skills
- Minimal legal formalities
- Pooling of capital
- Sharing of workload/pressure
- No public disclosure of accounts
- Taxed similarly to a Sole Trader

Disadvantages

- Jointly and severally liable for debts and liabilities of business
- Having to share control
- Limited access to capital
- Possible personality clashes
- Death of partner could dissolve business
- Need for a Partnership Agreement and clear exit route

Limited Liability Partnership

Advantages

- Limited Liability
- Protection of business name
- Start straightaway
- Pooling of skills
- Pooling of capital
- Sharing of workload/pressure
- Taxed similarly to a Sole Trader

Disadvantages

- Taxed as a Partnership not Limited Company
- Minimum two partners
- Accounts have to be submitted to Companies House - public disclosure
- More bureaucracy
- Possible personality clashes
- Death of a partner could dissolve the business if only one member left
- Need for a Partnership Agreement and clear exit route

Limited Company

Advantages

- Limited Liability
- Better public image
- Protection of Business Name
- Continuity of business, if Directors die - really cheery !!!
- Access to capital – issue shares
- Entitled to DSS State benefits

Disadvantages

- Cost of setting up higher
- Takes time to incorporate
- Tightly regulated
- Public disclosure of accounts
- Directors subject to PAYE tax
- Pay Class 1 NI contributions

CHAPTER EIGHT

LEGAL ASPECTS - PROTECTING THE BUSINESS

There are a number of aspects of running a business which you need to consider protecting from a legal point of view:

- your name

- your idea

- to be certain of getting paid

- to avoid being sued by customers or staff

- to obey the law/business regulations.

The Business Name

Choosing a name (the right name) for your business is a very important decision. It is equally important to then take steps to protect your name to ensure that someone doesn't later on start up using the same name, taking advantage of the 'goodwill' you have built up using that name.

One of my clients came to see me a few years ago who had created a Virtual Tour Travel web site, which was getting one million hits a month and selling lots of DVD's as a result. He was a Sole Trader and as such had not registered the name of the Virtual Tour. A well known big company chanced upon his site and produced their own version using the same name. He consulted a solicitor who advised that he had no case because he had used a combination of words already in use in the public domain and had not taken steps to protect the name. He could for example have registered the style of the name as a Trade

Mark and also formed a Limited Company, to give him more protection than just being a Sole Trader.

As a **Sole Trader or Partnership you cannot register your business name**, which used to be a legal requirement and gave you some protection.

If you intend to trade in a name other than your own, you should check with the Companies House web site (www.companieshouse.gov.uk) to check on the regulations you must satisfy in naming any sort of business (Sole Trader, Partnership, Limited Company).

There are restrictions on the use of certain words and disclosure requirements – e.g. you must show your trading title, your name and address on any stationery you have printed, as well as a notice (on or near the front door) with such details on any premises you occupy, other than your own home. People must be able to identify the owner of the business, behind the trading title, and have the address to where documents can be sent if they have a claim against that business.

You should also check with Yellow Pages (www.yell.com) to ensure that no-one is already using the name in the area in which you plan to trade, and that no-one has booked to use the same name in the next issue. You need to check before you have your stationery printed.

Again, another true story. When the film 'Ghostbusters came out, three ladies started up separate domestic cleaning companies in Oxfordshire and advertised in Yellow Pages, but the second and third business to register weren't told that someone had come up with the name 'Dustbusters' already.

When the Yellow Pages came out we had a phone call to ask what could be done. We told them that as Sole Traders they were not able to do anything unless they could prove they were the first – we suggested they explored amalgamation! Since then we have recommended that people send themselves an envelope with their trading name and address and get a dated Certificate of Posting. On that day they had that name.

As a **Sole Trader/Partnership** you can give yourself some protection by registering the logo or style of your name as a **Trade Mark**, for

96

example Coca Cola's trade mark is its name in a particular font style

There is a web site (**www.anewbusiness.co.uk), which offers you a facility to register your name as a Sole Trader/Partnership**. They will send you a certificate and state that they will take others to court who subsequently attempt to start up using your name, known as a 'passing off' action. The certificate on its own gives you no legal protection, and 'passing off' actions can be difficult to prove. You need to satisfy yourself that this service will give you the protection, particularly if you have a really good name and build up a great deal of 'goodwill'.

Anyone could stop you using your name if they successfully show that they used that name before you and the name is associated with their business – a 'passing off' action.

As a **Limited Company**, Companies House will register your Company name, which in effect means that they will not allow others to register using exactly the same name. This will not protect your Brand Name or Trading Name.

If you plan to have a web site at some stage you need to check that your **'domain name'** is available and then register it, even if you don't plan to have a web site straight away. The web site is (www.nominet.org.uk) giving availability and a facility to register the 'domain name'. If you are unsure, then seek advice from a solicitor.

*Intellectual Property – Patents, Copyright, Design, Trade Marks

The term 'Intellectual Property' refers to the expression of new ideas and the rights of the people who had them to exploit their ideas commercially and artistically. The rights cannot apply to the ideas themselves only to the material or artistic forms they take.

Examples of intellectual property are: inventions, drawings, computer programmes/software, photographs, books and magazine articles.

As with any property, owners have the right to benefit from their ownership, but ideas are much easier to copy or steal. Owners are entitled to defend those rights. These rights are

known as patents, copyright, design rights, registered designs and trade marks.

Patents

To qualify for a patent, an invention must be new and must involve some inventive step which is not obvious to an expert in the field. They must be capable of an industrial process.

They cannot be artistic creations, purely mental acts, plants and animal varieties or certain medical processes.

They have to be registered with the Patent Office. They must not have had prior public disclosure.

To register a Patent can be very expensive and before you set off to do this you can carry out a basic check on the Patent Office web site (www.ipo.gov.uk), to see whether your idea has already been registered.

> **REALLY PRACTICAL TIP You also need to carry out some market research to establish whether there will be sufficient demand for your new product or service. This will probably involve you revealing your idea to someone who could then pinch the idea.**
>
> **You need to have a 'Letter of Non Disclosure' drawn up by a solicitor, which the people must be asked to sign, before revealing your idea. Failure to do this could disqualify your invention from registration as a patent.**

Copyright

Copyright gives automatic protection, without registration, to new literary, artistic and other creative works, including computer programmes. This lasts for 70 years after the author's death, although sound recordings, broadcasts and typographical arrangements of published editions have shorter periods of protection.

*Design

Like Copyright a Design Right exists in the design of any aspect of the shape or configuration (whether internal or external) of the whole or part of an article. A Design Right applies automatically to original, non commonplace designs and does not have to be registered. It allows for prevention of copying, lasting 15 years from the end of the calendar year when the design was first recorded or an article to the design was first made or if an article is marketed within 5 years from the end of the calendar year in which its design was created, 10 years from the end of the calendar year in which it was first marketed.

In addition to automatic design right, novel designs can be registered with the Patent Office.

Registered Designs give added protection. In particular, someone would be infringing your registered design even if they created it themselves independently without copying it. You might obtain up to 25 years of protection by registration, though you would have to apply every 5 years for another 5 years extension. Again it is important to understand that there must have been no prior public disclosure. Letters of Non Disclosure must be signed when discussing your designs. Also mail copies to yourself, or a solicitor.

If in doubt as to whether to register, consult a Solicitor who specialises in Intellectual Property

*Trade Marks

A trade mark is 'any sign capable of graphical representation which can distinguish the goods/ services of one undertaking from another undertaking'. A mark must be distinctive. It can be registered with the Patent Office. (www.ipo.gov.uk). You can also check to see whether it is in use already.

If you have a really good logo and want to protect your 'brand image' then it is vital you register it as a Trade Mark. You can do it yourself online. The cost currently is £200(£170 online) plus an additional £50 if you want to cover more than one category of product or service. Get professional help from a patent attorney to be certain you are protected.

*Licences

Certain types of business/activity require a licence to operate, including nursing homes, childminding and day care nurseries, taxi services, hairdressers, pet shops, massage and skin piercing services, night clubs, food, drink and catering including mobile shops, credit brokering, debt collecting, waste management and scrap metal dealers. The use of computer software requires a licence – you are asked to tick a box, accepting their conditions before use on screen.

*Contracts and Terms and Conditions of Trading

It is absolutely vital that before you provide a product or service you agree with your potential customer your terms and conditions of trading. The same applies regarding purchase from your suppliers, especially if you are relying on that in order to fulfil your promise to your customer.

These take the form of a contract or a simple exchange of letters.

A contract is a business transaction enforceable in law, whether written or verbal. It constitutes an 'offer' by one party, an 'acceptance' of that offer by the counterparty and a 'consideration' – normally the price. Any statement made during verbal negotiations may be construed as part of the contract.

In supplying goods or services on credit, you will need to agree **'terms and conditions of sale'** prior to supply (when you quote).

The effective management of your cash flow and limitation of your liability (within reason) could depend upon these terms. It is generally good practice to have standard terms and conditions to cover the basic terms which apply to most of your orders. If you sell products, your terms and conditions should also include **retention of title terms** which aim to keep the products you sell in your ownership until you are paid and to protect your right to payment for them even as against your customer's liquidator or administrator. When quoting for a job it is important to attach your terms and conditions, asking the customer to sign and date their acceptance of your terms, prior to you taking any steps to start the supply.

You can also show your Terms and Conditions on the back of your invoices, but this should not be the first time the customer sees them. **The 'contract' is made at the offer and acceptance stage.**

Large companies often have their own 'Standard Terms and Conditions', which you may feel obliged to sign. Try to negotiate unduly onerous conditions, which could seriously affect you as a small business, but which a bigger company would not see as a problem.

*Data Protection

The Data Protection Act 1998 requires a business to register as a Data Controller if processing personal data about clients, customers. It is not required for business data such as the address.

'Personal Data' is information relating to a living individual who can be identified from the information. 'Sensitive Personal Data' refers to items such as religious beliefs, ethnic origin, mental/physical health. 'Processing' is anything to do with recording information, which must be accurate and kept up to date. It must be held for no longer than necessary and kept securely.

To check whether you need to register, contact Data Protection/the Information Commissioner on (www.ico.gov.uk)'. There is a simple check list to see if you need to register. The annual fee is £35.

Insurances

Insurance is an area often overlooked, mainly because of the expense of the premiums. Needless to say, the cost of not having insurance could be far greater. One claim against your business could close it down.

You may need to consider some of the following insurances:

- **Public Liability**

If people visit your premises, you are legally obliged to provide cover in case of accidents. This applies either to a service or a product you supply, which might cause damage, injury or sickness. Similarly you need cover when you visit other people's premises in case you damage their property.

Your household insurance policy may have a clause giving you 'Public Liability' in respect of your domestic activities, with an upper limit of say £1 million pounds. This may not be sufficient to cover you for your business activities. Check with your insurance company or an insurance broker.

- **Product Liability**

This will be needed in case your product (one you manufacture yourself) causes injury to someone or damage to another process while in use.

- **Employers Liability**

If you employ anyone, you are legally obliged to provide Employers Liability insurance for work-related injury or sickness.

- **Professional Indemnity (P.I.)**

If you provide advice to others, perhaps as a consultant, business adviser, trainer or financial adviser you need to have P.I. insurance against being sued for wrongful advice.

- **Use of Room/Equipment at Home/Car**

Provide a brief description of your business activities which unless you do something to increase the risk – i.e. inviting clients into your house or carrying out activities which could cause damage to your property, should not result in an increase in premium, for example, where you are carrying out normal office/clerical activities.

> **REALLY PRACTICAL TIP Ask them to acknowledge receipt of your notification, so that you have a letter on their headed paper noting the situation.**

- **Building Insurance**

If business premises are rented, insurance might be required under the terms of the lease. If your business premises are owned by you, insurances are advisable.

- **Keyman Insurance**

This protects the income of the business if a senior or key member of the staff is unable to work for a prolonged period, or dies. Premiums are high.

Please Note that the Paragraph Headings marked with Asterisks in this Chapter, contain some wording reproduced from the Cobweb Business Information Fact Sheets. (See Chapter 3 – Desk Research.)

Premises

There are few legal restrictions on working from your home but once you decide you need to have premises you need to be aware of a number of factors.

If you decide to rent you can get a bulletin from your local authority showing you what's currently available in the area, both public and private sector.

Once you have identified a suitable property you need to ask the landlord for a copy of the lease. This should be looked at by a solicitor. Watch out especially for taking on liability to return the property in a better state and condition than it is in when you first take on the premises. If your business is a company or a LLP and additional security is required by the landlord, try to limit this to a rent deposit rather than an unlimited guarantee (known as a surety).

These are some of the main things you need to consider and discuss:

- Licence or a Lease

- Term - How Long - Break Clause

- Landlord and Tenant Act 1954 – your rights to extend/renew

- Planning Permission – Use of premises: check with Local Authority

- Repairing Obligations

- Schedule of Condition when you take possession

- Schedule of Dilapidations when you leave

- Personal Guarantees (in case of Limited Company Directors).

REALLY PRACTICAL TIP Never enter into an informal arrangement with a friend to use part of their premises without checking the legal position/their lease. They may not have the right to sublet. You may have to move out and get all your stationery reprinted if the landlord objects.

CHAPTER NINE

EMPLOYING PEOPLE

Initial Considerations

You will probably decide to recruit someone because you are working all hours, getting stressed and doing a lot of things you realise you could delegate to someone else to do to free you up to do the things that make optimum use of your time and earning power.

It is vital that you do not recruit as a 'knee jerk' reaction. You need to draw up a **'Job Description' and a 'Person Specification'** (what Business Skills and Personal Attributes are you looking for). You need to be thinking in terms of not only what you want that person to do immediately but what you might want the person and the job to develop into in the future. Be wary of recruiting friends or relatives unless they fit the criteria and are the best candidates of the ones you interview. They are difficult to get rid of or sack if it doesn't work out.

Once you employ just one other person you commit yourself to certain legal responsibilities.

There is an excellent website (www.acas.org.ok) setting out these responsibilities, and if in doubt you should consult a solicitor.

- **Discrimination**

The need to be aware begins at the recruitment stage where you have to consider the words you use when putting together your advertisement. You must be careful to avoid making statements which could discriminate against particular people applying for the job.

When you interview candidates you must ask everyone the same questions, again, avoid asking ones which could discriminate, e.g. asking a woman – are you planning to start a family in the near future?

You must keep any notes you make during the interview for a period of up to 6 months. Interviewees have a right to see the records of their interview after the event, should they feel you have discriminated against them in favour of the person who you actually employed. There is no upper limit to awards made to an employee at an Employment Tribunal for Discrimination.

REALLY PRACTICAL TIP Beware, there are people who make a living reading Job Advertisements and writing to firms claiming that the wording of their advertisement 'discriminates' against them applying for the job. Some firms have been advised by their solicitor to send the claimant money to 'settle out of court'!

- **Terms and Conditions of Employment /Contracts**

Once someone starts to work for you, they must by law be given written Terms and Conditions of Employment within eight weeks of their start date.

These should include the following:-

- Name of Employer
- Name of Employee
- Starting Date of Employment
- Job Title & Description
- Hours of Work
- Details of Pay
- Holiday Entitlement
- Length of Notice
- Disciplinary Rules

- Grievance Procedure

- Sickness and Injury Procedures

- Pension Rights (see 'ACAS' website for latest legislation re. Employers Obligations)

The employee should read these and sign and date a copy, indicating their acceptance, and this should be kept in your files for at least a year after they leave.

A **Contract** should be used where you have employees who will have access to the more confidential aspects of your business methods and financial information. Clauses will need to be included over and above the basic Terms and Conditions to protect you. For example, if an employee leaves and sets up in competition with you, having been privy to your commercially confidential information and your list of customers and contact details.

Such clauses might include not being allowed to take customers with them, not being allowed to start to trade within a certain time or a certain distance radius after their departure. Consult a solicitor to ensure you have the right wording – you cannot use words which could preclude them from being able to earn a living.

- **Dismissal**

Tread carefully! If you wish to dismiss someone you must go through a procedure, to give the person the opportunity to rectify the reason for your dissatisfaction.

The procedure normally starts with a verbal statement of your dissatisfaction and a request for the person to improve their performance, improve their punctuality or desist from some unacceptable practice, within a given period.

Training may need to be offered; there may be a valid reason for regular lateness – domestic situation or sickness. People must be given the benefit of the doubt.

Make a note of the details of your verbal warning.

If there is no improvement then the employee must be invited to a meeting to discuss the situation and to bring along a witness. A written warning should be issued, once again giving the person a period of time to improve their performance or to cease unacceptable practices.

If there is still no improvement then you may terminate their employment, but only after following these procedures.

Always consult a solicitor at an early stage before taking actions involving dismissal/redundancy. The cost of getting it wrong could be very high.

Legislation applies to those employed for more than 1 year.

Compensation for unfair dismissal awarded by an Employment Tribunal can be very costly.

There are three types of dismissal:-

1. Summary – in cases of gross misconduct, such as theft.
2. Wrongful – if insufficient notice was given.
3. Unfair - unreasonable reasons for dismissal, e.g. the grievance disciplinary procedure was not properly followed.

- **Redundancy**

You should have objective criteria for selecting someone for redundancy. There should be a clear procedure for dealing with the process.

The 'Acas' (www.acas.org.uk) website spells out the criteria and what could constitute 'Unfair Redundancy Dismissal'.

- **Health and Safety**

As an employer, you can be held legally responsible for the safety of your employees. Refer to the Health and Safety Executive website (www.hse.gov.uk) for a check list and a facility to audit your operation.

If you employ **more than five people at your premises** you must **provide employees with a written statement of the health and safety responsibilities** of both employer and employee. In any event these responsibilities should be verbally explained to the employee and ideally signed as being understood.

A statement must be prominently displayed to include information on the handling of equipment, fire extinguishers and the first aid box.

CHAPTER TEN

FINANCIAL PLANNING

This is the part of starting up a business where most people's eyes glaze over, the 'too difficult to deal with' bit.

Unfortunately, unless you make an effort to try and understand it, to determine to seek advice, to get training in book keeping and monitoring your financial performance, you could place your business in jeopardy.

You can't leave it all to your Accountant – they can't be there all the time. They can help you, but the more help you ask for the higher their fees will be.

Capital Requirement

In determining the amount of money (capital) you will need, you should take into account:

1. **The start up costs**

2. **The costs of acquiring new assets**

3. **The costs of operation once the new venture is up and running.**

You will also need to **value existing assets** likely to be used – your car, computer, telephone, desk, chair, etc. Make a list of all these costs (see this chapter) this is known as your 'initial investment' or your 'capital requirement'.

Financial Terminology

It is important to understand what is meant by **'capital', 'revenue expenditure' and 'working capital'**, when budgeting, keeping accounts and, where appropriate, for tax purposes.

Capital Expenditure

Is that which is incurred in acquiring assets, e.g. equipment, transport, computers, tools (over £200), furniture, premises. Such expenditure is not normally set against the cost of the operation in the year in which it is spent, but is spread over a period of years. This is known as **'depreciation'**, where you need to spread the cost over the likely life span of the item, and in effect put aside such amounts(allowing for inflation) to replace the item. Your accountant should advise you on the number of years – cars are normally depreciated over 4 years, computers over 3 years and more robust items, such as furniture, over 5 years.

This item of expenditure in your accounts is disallowed by HMRC – the tax people. They will add the amount you have allocated as **Depreciation** back on to your Net Profit figure. **Instead they provide Capital Allowances** to claim against your profit. You have to work to their rules, not those of you and your Accountant. (See Chapter 12 - Taxation - Capital Allowances.)

Revenue Expenditure

Is that which is incurred in buying consumables or services e.g. purchase of stocks for resale, materials, fuel, insurances, rent etc.

This is set against the cost of operation in the year it occurs.

Working Capital

Is the funding required to meet the day to day cost of operations for items such as wages, acquiring stocks/materials and the provision of credit (revenue items not capital as such). This is a term likely to be used by your Bank Manager, asking what level of cash (working capital) do you need to pay your monthly outgoings. Whereas you should be able to provide all or part of your initial Working Capital requirements you will probably need overdraft support from your bank to cover this initial shortfall.

You will almost certainly need further support as demand on your Working Capital will increase as the business grows.

CAPITAL, REVENUE AND WORKING CAPITAL

1. CAPITAL ITEMS OF EXPENDITURE

Desk, chair, filing cabinet
Computer (hardware, initial software)
Telephone, Mobile
Photocopier, scanner, printer
Transport (purchase, lease premium)
Tools and Other Equipment
Premises (purchase, rental/lease premium)
Premises (initial building/conversion costs)

TOTAL CAPITAL EXPENDITURE

2. REVENUE ITEMS OF EXPENDITURE

Purchase of Stocks and materials for resale
Wages, salaries (of employees/directors)
Travel, subsistence (meals, refreshments)
Hotel Accommodation
Entertaining
Motor Expenses
- fuel
- insurance
- Road Fund Licence
- AA/RAC subscription
- Service/repairs/tyres
- MOT, car parking
Total Motor Expenses
Telephone calls, postage
Rent/rates (business premises)
Heating/lighting
Equipment - lease/rent
Stationery, Printing, Advertising
Insurances
Professional fees (accountants, solicitors)
Professional/trade subscriptions
Contingencies (allow for unforeseen costs which might arise)

Computer Consumables

Text books, journals, newspapers

Bank charges and interest

TOTAL REVENUE EXPENDITURE

3. WORKING CAPITAL

Stocks, materials – monthly requirements

Wages

Drawings– monthly requirements

Credit given to customers

TOTAL WORKING CAPITAL

This is not an exhaustive list but gives you the typical items in the different categories.

FINANCIAL FORECASTS

There are two financial forecasts you will need to produce to provide the figures to support the facts in your Business Plan.

1. **Profit and Loss Forecast**

2. **Cash Flow Forecast**

Each of these forecasts will require you to estimate what sales you think you will make each month (your Sales Forecasts/ Income) and what costs you will incur in making those sales, running your business (your Expenditure).

Sales Forecasting

Forecasting what sales you will make and when you will make them could seem to be the most difficult thing you have to do in putting together your first Business Plan. You have no historical trading information and will therefore need to use the information you collected as part of your market research.

You will remember that when doing your face to face market research, it was suggested that you always noted people's body language as well as what they were saying to you. (See Chapter 3 - Market Research.) **It is those conversations you had with real people, that you can now base your 'assumptions' – your best**

estimates of what might actually happen, who might buy, when they might buy and how much they would expect to pay.

It is not unreasonable for you to assume that many of the 'positive body language' people you talked to really meant what they said and indicated, and are likely to buy once you remind them through your advertising and promotional activities, once you begin to trade.

Then you need to make further assumptions about sales you might make to other people or businesses, as a result of your advertising; calling on further potential customers, doing mail shots and so on – but using the same assumptions based on the representative sample of potential customers you saw before you started.

It doesn't matter if some of your estimates are wrong, some will be right or nearly right.

Write down all these **assumptions** as your best (informed) guesses at a moment in time. For example: 'I think I can sell so much of each product/service in each month (don't forget to allow for seasonal fluctuations) to a particular sector of the population, type of business.' Then convert the unit sales into the income generated.

> **REALLY PRACTCAL TIP** Always write down your assumptions, the words you were thinking and the date when you 'invented the figures'.

Once you start to trade you can then look at your sales forecast figures and the assumptions you made and update them in the light of actual trading and see where you guessed correctly and where you guessed wrongly. **You are not cheating, you are just acting on better information.**

> **REALLY PRACTICAL TIP** Another way to check whether your estimates are feasible is to say 'how much could I sell if everyone knew about me and I had a full order book?'

'How much could I sell given that I have to eat, sleep, do a lot of unproductive things like driving to and from seeing people, answering telephone calls, and e-mails, administration, as well as making the sales – and there are only so many hours in the day?'

'What is the maximum sales/income I could generate – that's my 100% target, but at first I will start slowly and only achieve, say 5% in the first few months, gradually building up to 100% over, say, three years?'

Also, you will have to take into account **External Factors** which may affect your level of sales:

- Is your overall market expanding/declining?

- Is it affected by seasonal factors?

- Which economic factors most affect your market, including currency fluctuations?

- What local events, trends, plans will affect it?

- Will new technology have an impact?

- How do political changes influence your market?

- How will you react if someone opens up in competition with you?

Are you prepared for all eventualities? You will need a contingency plan – 'what will I do if such and such happens?'

Profit and Loss Forecast

Before starting a business, before buying initial stock, entering into leases or making firm commitments it is vital to know and to see, on paper, whether you are likely to be able to make a profit or at least break even and not lose money.

To find out you need to produce a Profit and Loss (P & L) Forecast (all Bank and other business planning packs/CD's contain P & L forecast formats for you to enter your figures – ideally two columns for each month – one for your 'forecast' and one for your 'actuals'). These can be loaded on to your computer from the Bank CD's, or a Business Plan format downloaded from the internet.

Your Profit and Loss Forecast is a 'paper' exercise – having money in the bank does not mean you have made a profit. It is **not** a reflection of when money will come in and go out – that is a Cash Flow Forecast. It will also serve to show you how much tax you may have to pay.

The major difference between a Profit and Loss and a Cash Flow forecast is the treatment of capital – and the timing/incidence of income and expenditure.

To produce your P & L forecast you will need to have worked out **your Sales Forecasts** (the value of sales), for each month as a separate exercise. These sales figures need to be entered into the Sales column in the Income section, taking a credit for the sales in the month in which you expect to make the sale, not take the money. If you are a cash business that is one and the same month.

Any **capital** you are putting into the business from your own savings or a loan is not shown as an item in the Income section of your P & L forecast, but shown as an Asset on the **Balance Sheet** (see later in this Chapter).

From the total income for each month (value of your sales) and in the next section of your P & L forecast **'direct' (variable) costs** you need to deduct the costs of making the sales e.g. stocks, materials, wages/salaries of sales staff, in the month in which you expect to incur the expenditure (not pay for the stock), to arrive at **a 'Gross Profit Margin'**. (Not all businesses will have direct costs, e.g. people using their knowledge, brain power and not having staff).

The 'Gross Profit Margin' is required to establish whether you are in line with the 'market norm' percentage. (See Chapter 4 – Marketing –Pricing) and have sufficient money to cover your 'overheads' (indirect/fixed costs) and to make a reasonable **'Net Profit'**.

All other items of expenditure (your overheads) are totalled for the year, and one twelfth of the cost entered each month. You are spreading these costs evenly over the year (regardless of when they will be paid out).

These two tables will show you how not to do it (Table 1), and how to do it to show the true profit/loss situation (Table 2).

Profit & Loss Example Incorrect Method

Table 1

Months	1	2	3	4	5	6
Sales	1000	1000	1100	1500	2000	2500
Less Variable/ Direct Costs Cost of Sales	500	500	550	750	1000	1250
Gross Profit	500	500	550	750	1000	1250
Less Overheads Insurance	1200					
Rent	600			600		
Motor Expense	50	60	40	50	50	50
Light & Heat Premises			150			250
Telephone			300			360
Wages	150	150	150	150	150	150
Depreciation	1200					
Net Profit/ Loss	(2700)	290	(90)	(50)	800	440
Cumulative Profit/ Loss	(2700)	(2410)	(2500)	(2550)	(1750)	(1310)

Has this business really lost £1,310 by the end of six months?

No! But what have they done incorrectly? They have not spread the overheads equally over the twelve month period.

See Table 2 for the correct answer: £50 Net Profit, not a Loss of £1,310

Profit and Loss Example Correct Method

Table 2

Months	1	2	3	4	5	6
Sales £	1000	1000	1100	1500	2000	2500
Less Direct/ Variable Costs Cost of Sales	500	500	550	750	1000	1250
Gross, Profit	500	500	550	750	1000	1250
Less Overheads Insurance	100	100	100	100	100	100
Rent	200	200	200	200	200	200
Motor Expenses	50	50	50	50	50	50
Light & Heat Premises	50	50	50	50	50	50
Telephone	100	100	100	100	100	100
Wages	150	150	150	150	150	150
Depreciation	100	100	100	100	100	100
Net Profit/ Loss £	(250)	(250)	(200)	0	250	500
Cumulative P/L	(250)	(500)	(700)	(700)	(450)	50
Net Profit £50						

Recording Value of Capital Assets – Balance Sheet

As regards 'capital expenditure' you need to make a separate list of the value/cost of purchase of your capital assets, e.g. car, computer, other equipment/tools.

This will also provide you with the information for **your Balance Sheet – the Value of your Assets.**

The **Balance Sheet** will also list the value of Loans/Capital invested and details of your Creditors (people you owe money to) and Debtors (people who owe you money). Your Accountant will advise how and when you need this statement.

The Capital Assets will help you to earn money over a period of years and so the cost is spread over the lifetime of the asset, or as agreed with your Accountant – this is known as **Depreciation.**

Example

List of Capital Assets

Car Worth £8,000, but only 50% used for business – Business Use Car worth £4,000.

Depreciation £1,000 a year for four years, or £83.33 a month for 48 months.

Computer/ Laptop/ Printer Worth £1,500. Depreciation £500 per year for three years, or £41.66 per month for 36 months.

Other Equipment Mobile/Phone, Desk Chair – worth say £400 or £100 per year for 4 years or £8.33 per month for 48 months

Total Assets Depreciation figure is £83.33 + £41.66 + £8.33 = £134.32 per month or £1,611.84 per year for three years and £91.66 in year four (plus at that stage the depreciated cost of a replacement computer).

You also need to put away equivalent amounts each month to replace these assets. This is another reason why you need to establish the **Depreciation** amount.

Assets are normally depreciated over four years (computers three years) and so you take one quarter (or one third for computers) of the value of your assets for the first year and total all items to arrive at an overall figure for depreciation for the year per month (see example above). As with other items of 'overheads', the year total is divided by twelve to arrive at the monthly total to be entered. Take advice from your Accountant as to the appropriate period of time.

As regards arriving at a Net Profit figure for taxation purposes, the HMRC will disallow the figure you put in for **'depreciation'**, they will add it back to your 'net profit' and instead give you a **'capital allowance'** on your capital assets.

Summary - Profit and Loss

As you start to trade you need to enter your actual income and expenditure in the 'Actual' column (downloadable Business Plans provide two columns per month – one for your forecasts and one to put in your 'actuals') using the same principles used in your original forecast. Spread your overheads over twelve months and taking a credit for income and a debit for Direct Costs in the month when incurred, to show whether you are in fact making a profit. It will show you where you need to take action. Maybe you need to increase your price, or reduce costs and unnecessary expenditure or perhaps work faster, or possibly a combination of some or all of these.

Cash Flow Forecasting

The second financial forecast you will need is the **Cash Flow Forecast**, to establish whether you will run out of cash at any stage, and thus need support from the bank in the form of an overdraft.

Failure to look ahead and agree with the Bank an overdraft could result in the bank 'bouncing' your cheques. If this happens your business is likely to fail (your suppliers will stop supplying and you will not be able to pay your other bills) – even if on paper you are making a profit.

Once again, Business planning packs from Banks or Enterprise Agencies, contain a separate sheet for producing your **Cash Flow Forecast**, with ideally two columns for each month – a **'forecast'** and an **'actual'**.

The 'Income' section should contain your monthly **Sales Forecasts**, estimates of when you think you **will receive payments for your sales** and any other form of income, including capital/loans injected into the business bank account.

The 'Expenditure' section should record your estimates of when and how much you think you will pay out of your bank account for the various items of expenditure.

Each month you need to take the total 'Expenditure' for the month from the total 'Income' amount to arrive at a **Surplus/Deficit**. This will be your **'Closing Bank Balance'**, which in turn becomes your **'Opening Bank Balance'** for the following month. The process is repeated with the resultant surplus or deficit for the month being added to or taken away from the Opening Balance to arrive at **a cumulative Closing Bank Balance for month 2 (year to date) and so on each month.**

Once you begin trading and using the figures from the 'books' (records) you need to keep (see Chapter 11 - Book Keeping) you can enter the 'actual' totals for each month against each individual category of 'income' and 'expenditure'.

> **REALLY PRACTICAL TIP** The headings of the columns in your Main Cash Book should be the same as those used in your Cash Flow forecast to facilitate the transfer of the information to the correct columns.

Every three months or whatever period you feel comfortable with you then need to review how your 'actual' results compare with your original forecasts and recast your forecasts in the light of actual trading.

Assumptions

> **REALLY PRACTICAL TIP** To help in reviewing both your Profit and Loss and Cash Flow forecasts, it is vital that you write down what you were thinking when you first created the figures. Without doing so you may not remember how you arrived at the figures in the first place.

Always date your 'Assumptions'

You need to write down, for example, why you think you will achieve sales for each month, from which customer and how much. You need to write down when you think you will be paid, e.g. some customers will pay you within a month, say 80%, but others may not pay you until after the 30 days you agreed, say the other 20%. Therefore, Sales (of say £1,000) made in month 1 will show as Sales (£1,000) in that month on your Profit and Loss forecast, but as income of £800 in month two and £200 in month three on your Cash Flow forecast.

You need to establish when you will pay out quarterly bills (perhaps the month after you receive them) and your suppliers if they give you a month's credit you will pay out a month after receipt of the supplies.

By looking back at the words, which will explain the figures, you can tell where you estimated correctly and where you estimated wrongly, and then acting on better information recast your future figures for the rest of the period.

Using the same figures we looked at in the Profit and Loss examples, this is what they will look like when the Cash Flow forecast is compiled.

Cash Flow Forecast Example

No. 1

Months	1	2	3	4	5	6
Income Cash Sales	1000	1000	1100	1500	2000	2500
Less Expenditure						
Purchases Stock	500	500	550	750	1000	1250
Insurance	1200					
Rent	600			600		
Motor Expenses	50	60	40	50	50	150
Light & Heat			150			250
Telephone / Postage			300			360
Wages	150	150	150	150	150	150
Net Cash Surplus/ (Deficit)	(1500)	290	(90)	(50)	800	340
Cum. Cash Flow Surplus (Deficit)	(1500)	(1210)	(1300)	(1350)	(550)	(210)

However if you have to give credit and the income comes in a month later this will give a very different picture, and the need for a greater overdraft, as Example No. 2.

Cash Flow Forecast Example

No. 2

Months	1	2	3	4	5	6
Invoiced Sales 30 Days Credit		1000	1000	1100	1500	2000
Less Expenditure						
Purchase Stock Cash / No credit	500	500	550	750	1000	1250
Insurance	1200					
Rent	600			600		
Motor Expenses	50	60	40	50	50	150
Light & Heat			150			250
Telephone/ Postage			300			360
Wages	150	150	150	150	150	150
Net Cash Surplus / (Deficit)	(2500)	290	(190)	(450)	300	(160)
Cumulative Cash Flow (Deficit)	(2500)	(2210)	(2400)	(2850)	(2550)	(2710)

Note:- There is no mention of the word Depreciation in a Cash Flow Forecast. If you buy Capital Assets e.g. equipment this will appear as an item in the Expenditure section as Capital Purchases and the amount spent recorded against the month purchased.

BREAK EVEN

Establishing the Break Even point (knowing at what level of sales you will stop making losses and start making a profit), is a vital financial management tool.

Why do you need to know?

- Firstly, the **Bank Manager** will want to know how long it is going to take **before you expect to start funding the Cash Flow of your business from your profits** (at first more will go out each month than comes in, for which you may need an overdraft, using their money).

- Secondly, you need to know each month **what level of Sales you need** to achieve to cover your overheads **(to Break Even) and thus begin making a profit.**

- As your business develops you will **need extra resources. Knowing how to calculate the formula to assess what increase in sales income is necessary, takes the emotion out of the decision ('I cannot afford to take someone on' – oh yes you could if you knew how to do the sums!) - see example later in this Chapter.**

- It is a tool **to assess the effects of increased/reduced costs on sales/ profitability.**

> ## The Formula for Calculating Break Even
>
> ### Fixed Costs/Overheads (£'s)
>
> ### Divided By Gross Profit Margin Percentage = Break Even Sales (in £'s)

Let's look at an example of calculating Break Even

Value of Sales (Turnover)	£50,000
Less Cost of Sales (Stocks)	minus £20,000
Gross Profit Margin	£ 30,000

Gross Profit Margin Percentage (%)	
(£30,000 as a percentage of turnover	
£50,000 is ……….) 60%	

Fixed Costs/Overheads	£10,000

Net Profit	£20,000

Formula (using the above figures)

Fixed Costs   =   £ 10,000   =   £16,666
Gross Profit   60%
Margin (%)

£16,666 is the level of Annual Sales needed on this turnover of £50,000 to break even (i.e. before you start making a profit (or Sales of £1,388.83 per month).

Using the Formula to assess the effect of taking on an extra member of staff:

Example

Taking on an Admin. Person at a cost of £8,000 salary (an additional overhead cost), using the formula and the previous example figures:

Fixed Cost (Overhead)	£8,000	
Divided by	---------	=£13,333
Gross Profit Margin (%)	60%	

Additional Sales of £13,333 will need to be made to cover the cost of an Admin. Person at £8,000 (say, £6 per hour).

Remembering that as the owner you will free yourself up by delegating some of your admin. work to give you time to earn at your rate – say £20 plus per hour.

CHAPTER ELEVEN

BOOK KEEPING

Once you are up and running and people start paying you money, you start paying your bills, and there seems to be money in the bank, you will start to feel that all is well in the world. If you have been busy, working all hours, you will keep putting off this chore – keeping records, 'Book Keeping'.

Failure to 'grasp the nettle' will probably result in problems which will negate all your efforts, so determine to get some training before you start to trade. It is vitally important to set aside some time at the end of each day, or first thing the next day, to enter the information in your books. Do it little and often, so that it does not become a great mountain you have to climb.

As time goes on you may decide this activity is not the best use of your time and employ a book keeper (at a lesser rate than you can earn doing the things you are best at). But you need to know how to keep the records, because you, not the book keeper, will be fined if mistakes are made and your tax return is wrong. You need to check your books.

The Profit and Loss and Cash Flow forecasts help you to monitor and manage the finances of the business by comparing your budget forecast figures against actual performance.

So it is essential that you keep an accurate record of your actual income and expenditure each month. **This is what is meant by Book Keeping.**

There are three sets of records (books) you need to keep:

- **A Main Cash Book**
- **A 'Sales Ledger'**
- **A 'Purchase Ledger'**

Each month every individual transaction needs to be recorded and allocated to relevant headings such as 'sales' and individual categories of expenditure, e.g. stock, stationery, travel costs, in **the appropriate 'Ledger' record**. This could be manually in an **Analysed Cash Book**, on **a spreadsheet**, or on **your computer using Microsoft Excel or Book Keeping software.**

You also need to keep supporting documentation, e.g. invoices, receipts. If you forget to get a receipt, make out a Petty Cash Voucher. Every time you sell something, you must issue an invoice or receipt (sequentially numbered) and keep a copy for your files.

If you have a 'till' operation the daily totals of different items of income are summarised in your records, rather than entering every single item you sold.

Keeping accurate and up to date records is also a legal requirement. They may be examined by HM Revenue and Customs at any time – with a potential fine of up to £3,000 – and have to be kept for up to six years.

Having completed the individual transactions in each of the three ledgers, the totals of each column need to be added up for the month and reconciled. That is, do the totals of the individual items of Income and Expenditure add up to the same total as the Bank column?

The monthly totals of each column for the actual income and expenditure items then need to be transferred to the 'Actual Columns' of your original Cash Flow and Profit and Loss Forecasts, to enable you to monitor your progress. Are you on target or do you need to take some action to increase sales or reduce costs? Are you making a profit?

Main Cash Book

A simple accounting system, in the form of a Cash Analysis Book or a computer spreadsheet, is probably the most suitable for a new venture.

This Ledger is used to record individual items you pay into or out of your business bank account; cheques, cash and items which are taken out of your bank account such as Direct Debits, Standing Orders, Bank Charges – the **Main Cash Book.**

Every item of Income or Expenditure (the figures) has to be entered in the Bank column and again on the same line in the appropriate column to analyse the type of Income or Expenditure. The date of the transaction goes in the Date column. A description of the item sold or bought goes in the 'Description' column and the Pay In Book No. / Cheque No. Is recorded in the P.I.B./ Cheque No. column.

Do not enter items you sell or purchase on credit in this ledger.

If you opt for a manual system, it is important to choose a Main Cash Analysis Book with sufficient columns to analyse the various elements of income and expenditure. Some items of expenditure can be banded together in one column, such as postage and telephone costs, all motoring costs, all items paid quarterly e.g. rent, utility bills to avoid the need for a multiple column Cash Analysis book.

Some books have an equal number of columns on each side of a double page spread, one side for income and the other for expenditure. Others have fewer columns for income, e.g. 5, and far more, e.g. 12, for the greater number of categories of expenditure.

> **REALLY PRACTICAL TIP Analysed Cash Books can be purchased from stationers, but make sure you buy one with the right combination of columns to suit your recording needs. Talk to your Accountant if in doubt.**

Suggested Column headings – Main Cash Book/Computer Spreadsheet

The columns starting on the left hand side of a double page spread should reflect those you used in your Cash Flow Forecast and in the same order for items of income and expenditure, to facilitate the monthly transfer of the actual figures to your original Cash Flow Forecast Sheet (Actual columns).

Income

Date - Description of Item – Invoice/ Receipt Pay In Book No. - Bank (total amount of invoice/receipt, including VAT where charged paid into Bank) - Cash Sales - Receipts (Cheques, BAC's) from Credit Sales – VAT (where registered for VAT) - Other Income (e.g. capital introduced).

Example - Income (Left hand side of double spread sheet, Analysed cash book).

Date	Description of Item	Invoice P.I.B. No.	Bank	Cash Sales	Receipts from Credit Sales	VAT	Other Income

Similarly, on the right hand side of the double page, list the headings for 'Expenditure' entries.

Expenditure

Date - Description of Item - Cheque No. Direct Debit - Bank (total amount paid out, inclusive of VAT), a separate column for VAT (See Chapter 12 if registered) and then columns for each of the main elements of expenditure e.g. Stocks /Materials, Wages, Rent/Rates, Heat/Light, Telephone, Travel, Motoring Costs, Advertising. (Net of VAT if registered).

Example – Expenditure (Right Hand Side of double spread, Analysed Cash Book)

Date	Description of Item	Cheque No. Direct Debit	Bank	VAT	Stocks Materials	Wages	Rent Rates Heat/Light Telephone

Month End – Main Cash Book

At the end of each month you need to rule off the entries in your **Main Cash Book** (leaving two or three lines below the last entry to allow for items which have gone **directly out of your bank account such as bank charges or direct debits).** These items need to be entered in your Main Cash book from your monthly Bank statement, or from your computer Banking web site – print out if you are using Internet Banking.

You need to total up each individual column ensuring that the sum of the analysed columns equals the total 'Bank' column for both Income and Expenditure. This will show whether you have missed making an entry twice, once in the Bank column and again on the same line in the column analysing the item of income or expenditure. If registered for VAT (see Chapter 12 - Taxation) it will also show whether you have recorded the items of income and expenditure net of the VAT element, which is recorded separately in the VAT column.

The monthly totals should be entered in the 'Actual' column of your Cash Flow forecast to enable you to monitor your situation.

Your monthly totals should then be repeated on the bottom line of the page, to be carried forward and accumulated with the second and subsequent months, to give you a 'year to date' figure.

Always start a new month on a new page.

Main Cash Book – example

Left Hand side of Double Spread sheet – Income

Date June	Income Details	Pay in Book No.	Bank	Product 1 Consultancy	Product 2 Training
1st	J. Smith Consultancy	001	750	750	
3rd	T.Brown Training	002	500		500
10th	A. Carter Consultancy	003	850	850	
25th	B.Taylor Training	004	450		450
Totals			2550	1600	950

Right Hand side of Double Spread sheet - Expenditure

Date June	Expenditure Details	Cheque No. Visa	Bank	Materials	Transport Costs
1st	Fuel	Visa	50		50
5th	Training Materials	010	40	40	
15th	Fuel	Visa	50		50
28th	Training Materials	011	50	50	
Totals			190	90	100

Sales Ledger – Credit Sales

All items you have Sold on credit and have yet to be paid for have to be entered into your Sales Ledger, using the columns showing the Date, Name of Customer, Details of Sale, Invoice No., Total Due, Analysis of type of product or service. Date by which Payment should be received.

Purchase Ledger- Credit Purchases

All items that you Buy on credit and have yet to pay for are entered in your Purchase Ledger, using columns showing Date, name of Supplier, detail of Item Supplied, their Invoice No., Total to be paid, Date when Payment Due.

> **REALLY PRACTICALTIP** These transactions need not necessarily be recorded in two separate manual Analysed Cash Books. There could be one book with the Sales Ledger items recorded in the front to middle part of the book, and the Purchase Ledger from the middle to the end of the book as your business starts to expand.

When you first start with just one or two Sales or Purchase Invoices a month they can just be kept in separate Ring Binders, separating those that have been paid from those yet to be paid/ received, rather than recorded in separate ledgers.

Once you are paid or pay for these items a further entry has to be made in your Main Cash Book, listing these same items as having been Paid Into or Paid Out of your Bank, showing the Cheque Number, Pay-in Book number, Details and Date of Transaction.

Using a computerised spreadsheet or bespoke book keeping software facilitates this process avoiding the need for duplicate entries. You just instruct your computer system to transfer the transaction to the right record.

Monthly Action with Sales and Purchase Ledgers

Monthly totals of the invoices you have recorded in your 'Sales and Purchase' Ledgers should be transferred to the **'Actual' column of your Profit and Loss Forecast**. Your items of Expenditure – your overheads should be spread evenly, e.g. if you have a quarterly bill for telephone you need to show one third of the total for each of the three months in your accounts. If the bill was £300 for the previous quarter, Jan – Mar, you would allocate £100 in your P & L Actual column for each of the three months, Jan £100, Feb £100 and Mar £100.

This particular aspect, the allocation of overheads, does require advice from your Accountant as some accounting knowledge is needed for it to be done correctly.

Bank Reconciliation

You must check that the **entries in your Main Cash Book, Spreadsheet** are correct by **comparing them each month with your Business Bank statement.**

This Reconciliation exercise should be carried out below the 'ruled off' entries of 'income' and 'expenditure', on your Cash Book, Spreadsheet, as follows:

- **Tick** the items which appear on both your 'Main Cash' Book/ Spreadsheet and the Bank statement (make sure the Bank statement includes all dated entries for the month).

- List any differences under two headings:

  (a) Items on statement not in cash book (e.g. bank charges, direct debits).

  (b) Items in cash book, not on statement (e.g. cheques paid in or paid out not yet presented or cleared - uncleared receipts/payments).

- Revise or update the Cash Book (i.e. enter bank charges, Direct Debits).

- Analyse the differences under three headings:

  1. Cheques paid into the Bank but not yet cleared – **'Uncleared Receipts'.**

  2. Cheques paid out not yet presented or cleared – **'Uncleared Payments'.**

  3. Petty Cash in Hand.

Investigate any differences, e.g. bounced cheques.

It is vital to do this exercise to show whether you have missed making entries in your Main Cash Book, or whether the Bank has made a mistake. If you cannot reconcile the differences between the two records, do not leave it in the hope that you can sort it out the following month. Have a break and revisit the figures when you are refreshed. Check the following month to ensure the 'Uncleared Receipts' and 'Uncleared Payments' have appeared on your next Bank statement. Investigate if not.

This whole exercise can be made easier if you arrange to have online banking facilities.

Petty Cash

For day to day incidental expenditure, such as car parking fees, stamps, small items of stationery, coffee/tea it is better to record these in a Petty Cash Book, keeping a Cash Float and receipts in a lockable box. When items are purchased get a receipt. The details of what has been spent should be entered in a Petty Cash Book – Date, Description of Item and analysed into different elements of expenditure.

Every week the entries in the Petty Cash Book should be reconciled with the receipts and the remaining cash float in the Petty Cash Box to ensure they balance. (You should have receipts and cash totalling your original float). There may be differences because you forgot to get a receipt (make out a Petty Cash Voucher if you can remember the details) or you may have paid for something out of your domestic funds and not reimbursed yourself from the Petty Cash float.

> **REALLY PRACTICALTIP Eventually the Cash Float will run out and you will have a batch of receipts. These should be stapled together, with a covering sheet stating 'Petty Cash Expenditure for the period (date of earliest receipt to date of latest receipt) Total £--- '. An entry needs to made in the 'Expenditure' section of your Cash Book, the receipts filed in the Expenditure file and a new float drawn from the Bank.**

Pay In Books/Cheques Book stubs

It is vital to record every individual item of income on the **back of the 'Pay In' slip** both 'original' and duplicate, when paying in cheques/cash, e.g. list individual cheques, cash amounts providing information on payee, description of product/service provided and amount.

> **REALLY PRACTICAL TIP This information will be your only record of individual items paid into the Bank for recording in your Main Cash Book, Spreadsheet. Make sure you ask for a big enough 'Pay In' book.**

Also record details of date, to whom paid, description of product/ service purchased and amount on your **cheque book stub/ counterfoil**. Again, this will be your only record of items paid for with cheques for entering into the Expenditure section of your Cash Book Spreadsheet.

Filing - Keeping Receipts/Invoices

You are required by HMRC to keep your records for up to 6 years, including every receipt, invoice, pay in book and cheque book counterfoils, bank statements.

You will need a filing system, keeping your receipts and invoices in separate files in respect of Sales and Purchases. Use a ring binder for each and divide them into two sections 'Paid' and 'Unpaid'. Keep your other items in labelled plastic folders in a box file.

Whenever you make a Cash Sale issue a receipt or an invoice (sequentially numbered). Put a copy in the 'Paid' section of the Sales file, marking it 'paid'. For a 'Credit sale', file a copy of the invoice in the 'Unpaid' section. As you receive payment, mark it 'paid' and transfer it to the 'Paid' section, filing invoices in numerical and/or date order.

Whenever you purchase anything keep the receipt or invoice and put it in your 'Purchases' file. Items paid for at the time of purchase go into the 'Paid' section and those paid later in the 'Unpaid' section.

When you settle the invoice, note the cheque No. or date of BAC's payment on the invoice. Number each receipt or invoice and file them in the 'Paid' section in numerical order.

Check the 'Unpaid' sections of both files regularly to ensure: 1. your customers pay you on time, and, 2. you pay your suppliers on time.

It is important to do your books daily, or certainly weekly, if you are not to lose track of money into and out of your Business Bank account.

You may decide it is not best use of your time and get someone else to do your books.

You must, however, know how to do books to check their work. You are legally responsible for any mistakes made by your book keeper and/or Accountant.

You need to use the information monthly to monitor whether you are making a Profit or a Loss and whether you are likely to run out of cash.

Computerised Book Keeping

You may prefer to keep your books using a computer software package, e.g. Sage Instant Accounting, Intuit QuickBooks and QuickBooks Pro, Regular and Accountant, Pegasus Capital Gold. **Check with your Accountant, as ideally it is sensible to have a package compatible with their software system.** They may even provide you with some basic training in the use of the software to ensure you present your information as they need it. You will need some advice or accounting knowledge in allocating your 'overheads' to produce the monthly Profit and Loss accounts.

Backing Up Your Records

It is vital to take a back-up copy on a USB every time entries are completed and for this to be stored in a fire proof box along with a hard copy/manual books in a separate fire proof box.

If your computer records are destroyed, HMRC will invent what business they think you have done and tax you accordingly and they can go back six years – so you need 'belt and braces' storage.

DEBTOR / CREDIT CONTROL

When you first start your business you may be tempted to give credit to customers who ask for it, particularly those buying lots of your products/services. They will pay cash for the first one or two purchases and may then lure you into their little trap of running up bills they have no intention of paying! Seek to ensure that no one credit customer accounts for more than 25% of your turnover. The loss of such a customer could bring you down.

You may hope that your suppliers will allow you credit when you first start. Until you have proved your credit worthiness that is unlikely.

To properly manage the finances of your business it is vital that you understand the importance of taking advantage of any credit you can obtain from suppliers. In effect you are 'borrowing' money from your suppliers to finance the 'cash flow' of your operation. **BUT**

DO NOT ALLOW YOUR CUSTOMERS THE SAME FREE BANKING SERVICE

This may seem a contradiction, but if you are obliged to provide credit to your customers make sure you do not provide better terms than you get from your suppliers. Ideally, seek to achieve a situation where you are paid by your customers before you have to pay your suppliers.

The Golden Rules

In giving credit to your customers or clients there are some 'Golden Rules'.

- **Obtain credit references in advance on customers** – two from other businesses they have dealt with and one from their bank. There may be occasions where you have to walk away from potential work when you are uncomfortable about the creditworthiness of the potential customer.

There is a very good web site to give you guidance (www. payontime.co.uk).

- If you don't like to ask but want to do your own checks, there are one or two Agencies who will provide credit references for a fee: Experian (www.experian.co.uk) and Equifax (www. equifax.co.uk).

- **Before approaching a Bank** for a loan or to open a Business Bank account you can obtain, for a fee, **a credit report on your own financial status** from the same web sites.

If you expect to have a regular requirement for credit checks then it might be worth your while registering with one of the Agencies.

- When quoting to provide a product or service make your Terms of Trade clear and ask customers to sign and date their acceptance of those terms. State your payment dates on your invoices and repeat the Terms on the back, particularly if they are comprehensive. Ask for a deposit where up front costs are incurred.

- Issue invoices the day you do the work, provide the service and then make sure they are accurate. Do not leave doing them until the end of the month. If your invoice is not accurate, or something is returned (and you do not issue a credit note), this will give customers a further excuse for late payment.

- If you issue a number of invoices to a customer in any month send them a statement at the end of the month listing the outstanding invoices, and repeating the date by which you want paying.

- Have a system for telephoning late payers – check your sales ledger weekly for overdue accounts.

- For all customers ensure that you have the contact name of the person handling your account. Get to know them. Find out when firms do their monthly 'cheque run', making sure that your invoice arrives in time.

- Be assertive – remember that it is your money but more can be achieved with 'sweet talking' than with being rude or unpleasant.

- If when contacting firms you are not getting satisfaction, go up a level to the boss of the last person you spoke to. Ask your purchasing contact for help. They may not be aware of the delays in the accounts department.

- As a last resort, suspend further deliveries or supplies and send a solicitor's letter.

- If you have to take someone to court you can use the '**Small Claims' service** for debts up to £5000, without using a solicitor. There is a Business Information Fact Sheet, **BIF037 A Guide to Using the Small Claims Court**, obtainable from Enterprise Agencies, Libraries, Banks to explain how to do this.

- If you are in a sector of the market where customers traditionally take a long time to pay, or you have to pay your staff weekly, and you only get paid some time after the event, you may wish to consider using a professional **Factoring, or an Invoice Discounting service**. (See Chapter 13 – Start Up Funding). **These services are** usually provided by subsidiaries of Banks.

CHAPTER TWELVE

TAXATION

Up until now, if you have been employed your employer deducted the Tax and NI contributions each month and sent off the money to Her Majesty's Revenue and Customs (HMRC). If you were a basic rate tax payer, with very little other income, you probably never saw a Tax Return and didn't need to know about tax.

In starting up and running your own business you are responsible for your tax affairs not your Accountant. You will get a Tax Return.

It is important, therefore, to understand these responsibilities and avoid fines, or in extreme cases, imprisonment.

Registration

You are required by law to advise Her Majesty's Revenue and Customs when you start to trade.

Within three months of starting to trade as a Sole Trader or Partner (i.e. Self Employed) you have to complete a form CWF1 and **make arrangements to pay Class 2 National Insurance contributions**. These forms can be downloaded or completed on line from the web site (www.hmrc.gov.uk). They can also be obtained from your local HMRC office.

As a Limited Company or Limited Liability Partnership you have to complete a Form CT 41G. This will normally be sent to your Company Registered Office address by your local tax (HMRC) office, once they receive notification from Companies House that you have registered. If it is not sent you need to apply for it or download it from www.hmrc.gov.uk and/ or complete it online.

All businesses have to register for **VAT** once their turnover reaches a stipulated level (see HMRC web site). You have to register within one month of reaching the turnover level for the preceding 12 months using **Form VAT 1**.

Different Taxes Payable

Self Employed

- **Income Tax on Net Profits**
- **National Insurance (NI) Class 2 and Class 4**
- **Value Added Tax (VAT)**

Sole Traders and Partnerships pay Income Tax on their net profits, inclusive of any drawings (money you draw from the business for your own use – pay).

You are able to deduct the Personal Allowance and Capital Allowances from the Net Profit to arrive at a figure upon which Income Tax is payable .

You also pay Class 2 and your business pays Class 4 NI contributions (this latter tax appears on the Tax Return as a further element of tax payable over and above income tax, for self employed people).

Limited Liability Company/Limited Liability Partnership

- **Corporation Tax on Net Profits (Companies)**
- **Income Tax on Net Profits – (Partners - Limited Liability)**
- **National Insurance Class 1 – Directors, Employees**
- **National Insurance Class 2 and Class 4 (Partners - Limited Liability)**
- **Pay As You Earn (PAYE) Income Tax – Directors, Employees**
- **Value Added Tax (VAT)**

Limited Companies pay Corporation Tax on their Net Profits, after salaries, wages and PAYE have been deducted.

Directors/Employees pay Income Tax and Class 1 NI contributions on their salaries.

Limited Liability Partnerships pay Income Tax on their Net Profits, inclusive of any drawings.

Deductions for Personal and Capital Allowances are as for Self Employment, as are the NI contributions payable.

Other Income

You should be aware that any other income you earn will be aggregated with your Net Profits and Gross Salaries. After deduction of Allowances tax is assessed at differing levels, from which tax deducted at source will be taken off to arrive at the tax payable.

Minimising Your Tax Bill – Tax Avoidance

Tax evasion is a crime but tax avoidance means legitimately reducing the amount of tax you have to pay.

A good Accountant can advise you on how to conserve most of your hard earned money by telling you what can be claimed and **when best to take certain actions – tax planning.**

Firstly, all legitimate expenses incurred 'wholly and necessarily' in running your business can be deducted from your gross income. A suggested list of these items can be seen at the end of this chapter.

> **REALLY PRACTICAL TIP When you first register you may be able to claim a refund of Income Tax (on your previous employment) already paid in that tax year. You may have to pay it back in tax at the end of your first year, but it will improve your cash flow in the meantime.**

If your husband, wife, or life partner is involved in the business, it may be beneficial to make them an employee and pay them a salary and deduct PAYE. The total amount payable will reduce your net profit and therefore your tax liability. Alternatively, as partners in a partnership two or more amounts of net profit are aggregated before the higher rate of tax is incurred. **Do the sums. Get advice from your Accountant.**

Dividends - As a Limited Company you can pay dividends to Directors from Net Profits once Corporation Tax has been deducted. These are not currently subject to further taxation, unless you are a higher rate tax payer.

REALLY PRACTICAL TIP Pay yourself a small salary (just above the Personal Allowance rate) and take the rest of your remuneration in dividends. DO GET advice from your Accountant to ensure this is your best course of action. You cannot pay dividends if you are making losses, if by doing so you make the Company insolvent. This depends on your level of Reserves.

Contributions to a Personal Pension Plan will also reduce your tax bill, as well as providing for your retirement. **Again, get advice from your Accountant.**

The timing of when you buy or replace Capital Assets is also important.

A good Accountant is someone who puts your interests first and should be able to save you tax.

Timing of Tax Payments

The Tax Year runs from April 6th to April 5th, the following year.

Accountants will generally advise Self Employed businesses to choose their accounting year to tie in with the Tax Year by choosing a year end date of March 31s (the tax people will treat this as if it was April 5th). There is also another school of thought suggesting that you choose an April 30th Year End to maximise cash flow as tax would be paid 11 months later. Check with your Accountant.

Limited Companies could also do this but may need to take into account seasonable trading aspects, for example avoiding a year end when they have large stockholdings, or are having to renew capital assets at a less favourable time tax-wise.

Self- Employed people i.e. Sole Traders and Partnerships do not have to deduct and pay tax monthly, although they do have to pay their Class 2 NI contributions (quarterly, or monthly by Direct Debit).

Income Tax on your Net Profits is payable to HMRC, in a lump sum, on your first year's trading (ending on 31st March/April 5th) by the following January 31st.

By then your business will be well into its second period of trading, with just two months to go before the end of this period of trading. **So as well as handing over your first year's tax, you have to make an 'on account' payment on that first January 31st, for the current (second) trading period, in effect for the first six months (April to September 30th).**

Because you still have two months to go you cannot accurately forecast how much tax you might have to pay for this second period and so HMRC suggest you base your taxable profits at the same level as your first period of trading (allowing for the fact that you need to pro rata up the amount if your first period was for less than a year – see example below).

A second payment (for the second period of trading), then has to be made on the following July 31st. Each of these payments is deemed to be 50% of the 'assumed' amount of tax to pay for this second period.

In the event that your second year is better than your first period then you have to make a third payment of tax (a 'balancing' payment) on the following January 31st.

This is why it's probably very sensible to pay an Accountant to sort this out!

It is also why it is vital to have available up to date records/ books.

Example for Self Employed Sole Traders/Partners

<u>First Period of Trading</u> July Current Year (A) to March 31st Following Year (B), i.e. 9 months.

Net Profits on this period, say £4,000, 20% Tax, say £800*, payable on January 31st (Year C).

<u>Second Period of Trading</u> April Year (B) to March 31st Year (C).

Net Profits assumed to be £5,000 (i.e. £4000 pro rata for12months trading). 20%Tax Payable is therefore £1,000 of which 50% (£500**) also payable on January 31st Year (C). Actual Profits (2nd period of trading), say £8,000, Tax £1,600***.

<u>First amount of Tax</u> payable on January 31st (Year C) is £800* (i.e. first year), plus £500**, i.e. 50% of second period (assumed to be the same as your first period of trading) on account = £1,300.

Second Payment on July 31st Year C is £500 (i.e. 50 % of second period on account).

Balancing Payment on January 31st Year D is £600*** (i.e. balance of actual tax payable on second period of trading).

PLUS an 'on account' payment of tax for 3rd Year Trading – assumed to be 50% of Tax payable for second year, e.g. £800, also payable on January 31st Year D and so on.

You are always paying over your tax in arrears and so providing you put away the money every month, in an interest bearing account, you will have the tax there to hand over.

If your eyes glazed over going through this you certainly need to use an Accountant!

Table showing above information in tabulated form

Period of Trading	Net Profits £	Tax Payable £	Date Tax Payable
First Year 'A' July - March 31st Year 'B'	4000 (9 months - Actual)	800 - i.e. 20%	31st January Year 'C'
Year 'B' April - March 31st Year 'C'	5000 (Assumed to be the same as the first year - pro rata)	500 500	31st January Year 'C' 31st July Year 'C'
Year 'B' (Actual Profits)	8000 (20% Tax = £1600)	600 (Balancing Payment)	31st January Year 'D'
Year 'C' April - March 31st Year 'D'	**8000** (Assumed to be the same as the previous year	800 800	31st January Year 'D' 31st July Year 'D'
Further Balancing Payment	**If Actual Profits in excess of assumed level of £8000 due on Jan 31st Year 'E' and so on !!!**		

Limited Companies have to hand over their Tax as follows:

Income Tax and National Insurance contributions on their salaries and wages have to be handed over monthly in line with PAYE requirements.

Corporation Tax is payable on Net Profits nine months and one day after the end of the first period of Trading, although the Tax Return has to be submitted within twelve months of the end of the first period of Trading (estimates can be paid but if tax has been underestimated the balance payable must be sent off without delay).

Tax Rates

The up to date tax rates are published on Her Majesty's Revenue and Customs web site (www.hmrc.gov.uk).

The main ones likely to affect people running small businesses are as follows:

- **Income Tax** - There are currently two categories a Basic Rate payable on a band of income in excess of the Personal Allowance, and a Higher Rate payable on Income in excess of the 'Basic Rate' band of income.

Income Tax is charged on Net Profits of Sole Traders and Partnerships and on the Gross salaries and wages of people who are employed, through PAYE.

- **Corporation Tax** - This is the tax payable by Limited Companies on their Net Profits. There is a Small Company Rate and a Main Rate of Corporation Tax.

The Small Company Rate is applied to Net Profits up to a certain limit, before the Main Rate is applied. This compares with a much lower ceiling for the Basic Rate for Self Employment before the Higher Rate is applied to Net Profits in excess of the Basic Rate. See the HMRC website www.hmrc.gov.uk for current rates.

Allowances

Taxes are applied after the deduction of **Business Expenses Allowances** from Gross Income, i.e. on Net Profits. The **Personal Allowance** (this is the amount we are allowed to earn Tax Free before taxes become payable), is also deducted from Net Profits, but not additionally if it is already being deducted from some other form of income.

Further amounts, **Capital Allowances**, are deducted from Net Profits to arrive at a (Net of Net) Profit upon which taxes are charged (Income, Corporation).

- **Business Expenses Allowed**

A list of the typical items of allowable expenditure (the HMRC definition is 'expenses which are incurred wholly and necessarily in running the business') is shown at the end of this chapter. Allowable expenses will depend on the type of business - a training company might justify a lap top and projector as a business expense, but a garage owner could not justify the projector.

It is important to check with your Accountant as to what can and cannot be claimed and other areas, such as tax efficient pension funds, company loans, leasing, which could help to minimise your tax bill.

- **Non Allowable Business Expenses**

Personal or domestic expenditure (this should be met from your Drawings or Director's Salary/dividends).

Taking business stock for personal use.

Personal Drawings (deemed to be an integral part of your Net Profits).

Entertaining expenses (you may entertain customers but you cannot claim).

Depreciation on your Capital Assets (e.g. car, equipment etc.).

- **Capital Allowances**

Depreciation (the amount you deduct from your Income/Gross Profit, to reflect the annual cost of replacing your assets), is a Non Allowable Business Expense. You can show it in your accounts, but it will be disallowed by HMRC, who will add the amount of Depreciation back to your Net Profits and instead allow you a **Capital Allowance (also known as a Writing Down Allowance).** This is deducted from your Net Profit to arrive at a lower figure upon which tax will be charged.

The current Capital Allowances are listed on the HMRC web site (www.hmrc.gov.uk).

Self Assessment

In registering with HMRC, either as a Self Employed person or a Limited Company, you will automatically be sent a Tax Return early in April, or it will be sent to your Accountant if you indicated that they would be handling your tax affairs – your Agent. You will also get a form to complete if you were employed in the period leading up to your self employment .

If they do not arrive, get in touch with your tax office to request the forms. Do not ignore in the hope that you can avoid paying.

You are required to complete this return manually or you can complete it on line and pay your taxes as follows:

- **Self Employed**

The return must be completed, in respect of the previous year's trading ending April 5th (up to March 31st accounts), and sent off to HMRC, or transmitted online by the following December 30th, if you want HMRC to work out what tax you owe, which then has to be paid over by the following January 31st. They will send you a statement showing the amount payable.

Alternatively, you have until January 31st to complete your tax return and work out what tax you owe and then pay it. The Guiding Notes you are provided with are copious. If you get it wrong you may end up not paying enough and could be fined.

- **Limited Company**

The Tax Return has to be completed within 12 months of the ending of the first period of trading, but the tax payable for that period has to be paid within nine months and one day after the end of the trading period.

It is advisable (and for a Limited Company vital at all times) to use an Accountant, to ensure that you do not over or under estimate what tax is payable. Under estimation could lead to fines and other penalties.

Tax Evasion

With the advent of Self Assessment the HMRC have more time to investigate where they suspect that business owners have not declared all their income. Over the years I have heard a number of examples from Accountants, who came along to my training courses to tell people about Taxation and the various things the Tax people do to track down non-payers.

One such case was a client of an excellent Accountant, who ran his local business and paid all his taxes. Unbeknown to the Accountant his client also sold second hand cars as a side line, but did not tell the Accountant or declare the income.

The Accountant was invited to the office of his local HMRC and was shown page after page of photocopied entries in the local weekly paper highlighting his client's home telephone number in the Used Car advertisements.

HMRC not only taxed the client on these sales but also fined him a similar amount. They also investigated where the client had got the money to finance the purchase of these cars – a friend who owned three businesses, who in turn was fined and taxed, ending up with just one business.

What triggered the investigation was that the wife of the local Tax Inspector had bought a second hand car from this man, who when asked to provide a receipt for the money paid said 'We don't give receipts'!

So PAY YOUR DUES!

National Insurance Contributions

In addition to Income Tax and Corporation Tax you will have to pay National Insurance (NI) contributions. **The current rates are shown on the HMRC web site (www.hmrc.gov.uk)**.

- **Self Employed**

There are two categories of NI contributions payable by the Self Employed.

Class 2 – this is a weekly payment, which can be paid monthly by Direct Debit or quarterly by the Owner, Proprietor, Partner, once annual Net Profits exceed the Personal Allowance. This entitles you to a limited number of benefits – mainly the Health Service and an Old Age Pension. It does not entitle you to Job Seeker Allowance (Contribution based), if your business were to fail; nor does it entitle you to benefits such as Statutory Sick Pay and Maternity, or Paternity benefits. This is basically because the weekly premium is much lower than that paid by an employee/employer – Class 1 NI.

Class 4 – this is a further tax payable by the Self Employed. It is a straight tax payable on Net Profits in excess of the Personal Allowance and with an upper ceiling similar to the Basic Rate of Income Tax.

This appears on the Tax return and needs to be put aside each month and paid with the Income Tax.

- **Limited Companies**

Class 1 NI contributions have to be paid by Company Directors and employees and people employed by Self Employed businesses. There are two elements – a percentage of the Salary/Wage payable by the Employer (Employer's Contribution) and a second slightly lower percentage paid by the Employee (Employee's Contribution). If you are a Company Director you are of course both the Employer and an Employee and have to pay both elements on your salary.

The current rates are shown on the HMRC web site. The money has to be paid by the following month as part of the PAYE scheme.

Class 3 contributions are Additional Voluntary Contributions (A.V.C's) which you can elect (whether you are Self Employed or a Company) to pay on top of other contributions, to maximise the State Pension when you reach retirement age. This is only if you are likely to have not paid contributions for the requisite number of years. Men traditionally have had to pay 44 years of contributions and women 39 years (to qualify for a full State Pension at 65 and 60 respectively), but this has been reduced to 35 qualifying years. The current rates are on the HMRC web site.

> **REALLY PRACTICAL TIP You can check with the Contributions Agency (part of HMRC) to establish how many years have been credited to you at any stage and what you need to pay to be eligible to get the full pension. As a mother your State Pension contributions should have been made as part of the Child Allowance you received, but check anyway.**

Value Added Tax (VAT)

Registration

If you expect your annual turnover to exceed the minimum figure set by the government in the Budget you must register for VAT. **The current limits are shown on the HMRC web site.**

If you do not exceed the limit in your first twelve months it does not mean that you need not register for another twelve months.

Each month thereafter you need to establish whether you have reached or exceeded the limit in the preceding twelve months – i.e. on a 'rolling basis'.

You have one month after reaching or exceeding the limit to register, using the Form VAT 1, downloadable from the HMRC web site.

You will be given a VAT registration number and this must be shown on all your invoices.

> **REALLY PRACTICAL TIP Ask to obtain a VAT Quarter End that is co-terminus with your Year End. For example if your Year End is March 31st you want VAT Quarters which end June 30th, September 30th, December 31st March 31st.**

Failure to register on time will lead to having to pay HMRC for VAT you haven't charged or collected.

Recording VAT Transactions

Once registered every time you receive a payment for goods or services the VAT element must be recorded separately (on invoices, receipts and in your books) and later paid to HMRC on a quarterly basis. Any VAT you have paid on items you have purchased must also be recorded separately and VAT receipts retained and can be offset against the amount you pay HMRC.

REALLY PRACTICAL TIP If you only deal with other VAT registered businesses you can opt for voluntary registration, even if your turnover does not exceed the minimum limit.

This will allow you to reclaim the VAT paid on all your business purchases. You can also claim back the VAT on any assets you use in your business which you purchased in the preceding three years, providing you still have a VAT receipt in respect of the purchase. This would also apply to any remaining stock, adverts or insurances still current.

REALLY PRACTICAL TIP If you deal with members of the public only or a combination of this type of customer and VAT registered businesses you may be tempted to register for VAT even though your turnover is below the VAT registration limit. Whilst this will give you the advantage of lower costs it will also make you more expensive (by the VAT rate) than your competitors who are not registered and provide services and products to members of the public only. You need to do the sums and consider the pros and cons.

The amount of VAT you charge your customers is known as **Output VAT.**

The amount of VAT you pay your suppliers is known as **Input VAT.**

Completing a VAT Return

Once registered you will be sent a reminder e-mail to complete a VAT Return form online every three months. The main information you have to provide is:

1. Total amount of VAT for the previous three months **(quarter)** charged to your customers on sales – **Output VAT.**

2. Total amount of VAT for the previous three months paid on purchases – **Input VAT.**

3. The difference between these two amounts **Sales minus Purchases** which you have to pay to HMRC or if claiming back amounts of VAT paid on business assets purchased prior to registration – the amount you are reclaiming from HMRC.

4. **The total value of your Sales for the quarter excluding VAT.**

5. **The total value of Purchases for the quarter, excluding VAT.**

Other boxes on the return refer to sales or purchases made in the EU which can be left blank if you only trade in the U.K.

The form has to be completed and the amount of VAT due paid within one month of the end of the quarter. There are penalties for late submission.

Cash Accounting

If you invoice your customers for products or services you may find that you may not have received payment for these, including the VAT, by the end of the quarter (usually for those invoices issued in month 3 of the quarter).

To avoid having to pay over VAT that you have yet to receive from your customers you can elect to pay HMRC using the **'Cash Accounting' system**, i.e. at the end of each quarter you declare on your form **only** the VAT you have charged and received and also **only** the VAT you have paid for purchases and the corresponding Value of Sales and Purchases.

Invoices for VAT you have yet to receive or pay for must be included on the next quarter's return. Accurate records must be maintained to ensure you don't miss declaring this information or double recording or paying.

Flat Rate Accounting

Instead of the need to record the amount of VAT you charge your customers and separately the amount you pay on your purchases in your books, you can elect to pay the **Flat Rate**. This is a percentage, which is **variable for different** categories of business.

These are listed on the HMRC web site and in effect reflect the averaged out net amount between the value of VAT charged to customers and paid out on purchases, expressed as a percentage of the value of sales for each category of business.

> **REALLY PRACTICAL TIP You need to do the sums to see whether the Flat Rate is the most beneficial to your pattern of business sales and purchases. It works for certain industries but not others. Check with your Accountant.**

Different categories of VAT

There are currently 3 different categories:-

- Standard Rate – most goods and services
- Zero Rate – food, children's clothes, newspapers, books, passenger transport
- Reduced Rate – domestic fuel, installation of energy saving materials, residential conversions

It is vital to seek the advice of your Accountant when considering whether to register for VAT, and also once you have registered. The various rules are not straightforward and interpretation from **an expert is highly recommended.**

HMRC can and do send in inspectors to businesses from time to time, who will require to see all your records and paperwork. **Ignorance of the rules is no defence.**

Items of Cost Which May Be
Claimed by the Self Employed

Cost of Goods Purchased (after adjusting for stocks)	£ x.xx
Cost of Materials used (after adjusting for stocks)	£ x.xx
Subcontracted Labour	£ x.xx
Wages and Salaries	£ x.xx
Secretarial Services of Spouse/Partner	£ x.xx
Commissions Paid	£ x.xx
Protective Clothing	£ x.xx
Loose Tools	£ x.xx
Business Use of Home	£ x.xx
* Entertaining	£ x.xx
Travel and Subsistence, hotel accommodation, meals	£ x.xx

Motor Expenses - petrol, oil, repairs	£ x.xx
Insurance	£ x.xx
* Hire Purchase	£ x.xx
Road Fund Licence (Tax)	£ x.xx
AA/RAC Subscription	£ x.xx
Total	£ x.xx

Business Proportion Claimed	£ x.xx
Car Parking, Car Wash	£ x.xx
Taxis/Trains/Air Travel	£ x.xx
Telephone (business proportion)	£ x.xx
Professional/Trade subscriptions	£ x.xx
Insurances – Public/Employers Liability/general/PI.	£ x.xx
Advertising, Promotion	£ x.xx
Hire of Equipment	£ x.xx
Repairs, renewals and maintenance of equipment	£ x.xx
Typing and Photocopying	£ x.xx
Postage, Printing and Stationery	£ x.xx
* Computer Software	£ x.xx
Computer Consumables	£ x.xx
Newspapers and Magazines	£ x.xx
Text Books and Journals	£ x.xx
Accountancy Fees	£ x.xx
* Legal Fees	£ x.xx
Discounts Allowed	£ x.xx
Bad Debts – specific	£ x.xx
Bank Charges and interest	£ x.xx
Contingencies	£ x.xx

Items marked with an Asterisk

- Entertaining is an item of expense which can be shown in your accounts but is disallowed as a tax deductible item.

- Hire Purchase. The Interest element only of the monthly payment is tax deductible. The Capital element is subject to the Capital Allowance Tax rules.

- The Legal Fees in connection with the acquisition of a Capital Asset are treated as part of the Capital Expenditure and subject to the Capital Allowance Tax rules.

This is not an exhaustive list – check with your Accountant.

CHAPTER THIRTEEN

START UP FUNDING

To start up your own business you will need enough money to set up and to cover your initial operating costs. You may have savings to cover your initial needs but not enough to then develop the business.

There are a number of **Sources of Finance** for small businesses:

- **Banks**

- **Credit Cards**

- **Factoring/Invoice Discounting**

- **Asset Financing**

- **Leasing**

- **Hire Purchase**

- **Family and Friends – Loans, Equity**

- **Local Venture Capital Investment Networks**

- **Business Angels**

- **Royal British Legion**

- **The Princes Trust – Business**

- **Livewire**

- **Prime**

Banks

It is vital to have a separate Business Bank Account when starting a new business. With the present economic situation, it will pay to shop around to compare the various Business Banking services available from Banks.

Loans

Banks provide Business Loans to acquire assets. The loan is usually secured against the asset, but in the case of larger amounts the bank may require to secure the loan against a personal asset such as your house. Interest is charged and the term of the loan should ideally be linked to the expected life of the asset.

Mortgages

Commercial Mortgages are typically used to buy premises. They are usually secured against the premises and are repaid over longer periods than a business loan, with traditionally lower interest rates.

Overdrafts

These are used to finance short term trading cash flow requirements (working capital), to cover periods of time when more has gone out of your bank account than has come in. They are repayable on demand, and you only pay interest when you are overdrawn. As with bank loans you pay a set-up fee, which is payable every time the level has to be reviewed and changed.

The Bank will need to see your Cash Flow Forecast to assess the maximum level of overdraft support you might need. When you first start up you might want to produce two forecasts – one showing the situation if your sales forecasts are achieved and the second one showing what would happen if you only achieved, say, 50% of your sales forecasts. Your cost of sales would reduce, but your overheads would remain the same and thus there would be a greater level of overdraft needed.

An experienced Bank Manager will see whether you are being too optimistic with the first, or too pessimistic with the second.

Credit Cards

Like personal credit cards, a business credit card allows you to purchase items up to an agreed limit and to spread the repayments over a period of time, with interest payable on monthly outstanding balances. The rates are usually higher than those payable on loans or overdrafts.

If all your business purchases are made using the business credit card it will facilitate your book keeping process.

Factoring and Invoice Discounting

If you are in a type of business where traditionally your customers take a long time to pay you, then Factoring and Invoice Discounting are financial services which will be of great benefit to you. If you pay staff weekly for providing a service to your customers for which you are paid monthly, or possibly longer (e.g. an employment or care staff agency), this service will help you. It is available from banks.

Basically, the **Factoring service** advances you up to a certain percentage of your approved invoices (about 75%). This is credited to your bank account shortly after individual invoices are sent to the customer, thus improving your cash flow by not having to wait to be paid by the customer. They are, in effect, lending you money against the value of your individual invoices on which interest is payable. They will only allow this facility against customers they have credit risk assessed.

You raise the invoices and send them to the customer with a copy to the factoring service. The factoring service then collects the payments and sends you the money less their fee and the interest payable. You need to compare the cost with those charged for an overdraft.

Invoice Discounting is similar to factoring but the lender provides a facility against the overall outstanding sales invoices. There is a monthly fee and interest is charged. Your customers pay you directly and are unaware of this facility.

Asset Financing

There are two types of asset financing – **Leasing and Hire Purchase. Leasing** is where you have use of the asset, but return it at the end of the period. The leasing costs can usually be set off in full against your income, unlike the capital cost of assets which you own or purchase, which are subject to capital allowances.

Hire Purchase enables you to purchase an asset over a period of time, with the purchase being secured against the asset acquired. The asset becomes your property once payment is made in full. The capital element of the repayments is subject to capital allowances and the interest element is treated as a tax deductible cost.

Family and Friends

If you cannot get a loan from a bank, you may be able to borrow from family or friends on preferential terms – lower or no interest. However, if you pay interest you will need to get advice from an accountant on the tax implications for both parties.

There is also the risk to your personal relationships, if your business does not do well and you cannot repay them on time or in full.

Family or friends may alternatively consider investing their money in your business in return for a share of its ownership, by either taking an active part in the business or as a 'sleeping partner'. Like all investors they have to understand they will be risking their money and that you are not guaranteeing to pay them dividends, or that they will make a profit from their investment.

This can only happen if you form a limited company (not a Sole Trader or Partnership) and you need to take advice, again, from an Accountant.

Venture Capital/Business Angels

This is another form of finance where a part of your business share capital – or equity – is sold in return for a cash investment, which means you have to surrender part of the control of your business.

Venture Capital businesses generally are looking to make larger investments (£1 million+).

Business Angels are private investors, who have made money from their own successful business, who look for other opportunities to invest in new or growing businesses. **You may have seen 'Dragon's Den' on T.V. Hardly angelic you may think!**

Generally speaking venture capitalists, business angels, will only invest in businesses with a winning idea and with a business owner who has a range of management skills or access to such expertise. **There are business angel matching services which can be accessed through the internet: (www.bbaa.org.uk)**

Other Sources of Funding

Royal British Legion

- Interest free loans to unemployed ex-service men and women - up to £7500.

  Contact (**www.britishlegion.org.uk**) – **poppy funds/small business loans.**

The Princes Trust – Business

- Grants, loans and practical support for both unemployed, underemployed and disadvantaged people under the age of 30, to help start up their own business.
- Grants up to £1,500, in special circumstances
- Test Marketing Grant – up to £250
- Low interest loans of up to £5,000

  Contact (**www.princestrust.org.uk**)

Shell Livewire

- Free start up advice and annual competition for 16–30 year olds – must have been trading for three months at time of deadline for entries normally January 31st each year.

  Financial prizes and publicity at local, regional and national level.

  Contact (**www.shell-livewire.org**)

Prime Initiative

- A scheme also founded by Prince Charles to help people over 50 to set up in business.

  Contact (**www.primeinitiative.org.uk**)

CHAPTER FOURTEEN

OTHER CONSIDERATIONS

STRENGTHS AND WEAKNESSES, OPPORTUNITIES AND THREATS (SWOT) ANALYSIS

This form of Analysis is a basic management technique which is designed to help you identify the Strengths, Weaknesses, Opportunities and Threats which face your business.

It is important to compare the strengths and weaknesses of you and your business with those of your competitors and how they will affect your overall performance. It is important to consider undertaking training in those business skills in which you are not so good.

S - STRENGTHS

- The things you are good at that your customers will value
- The things that make you different
- Areas of particular strength or skill e.g.:
    - Years of experience
    - Excellent marketing Sales
    - Well organised
    - Attention to detail in providing service

W – WEAKNESSES

- The things you know will let you down
- The things that hold you back e.g.:
    - Poor marketing sales
    - Dependence on too few customers
    - Lack of certain skills

O – OPPORTUNITIES

- Changing market needs which you can meet with existing skills expertise
- New groups of potential customers
- Improvements in technology
- Opportunities to export

T – THREATS

- The risks you face - illness, bad publicity, accident
- Loss of key customers
- Other competitors starting up
- Staff leaving to join competitors
- Financial changes

As you do your Market Research it is important to be thinking about these four areas as you gather information.

> **REALLY PRACTICAL TIP As mentioned in Chapter 3 - Market Research, it is very useful to do a written matrix showing the Strengths and Weaknesses of each of your competitors. Add your business, so that you can see on paper where you are better than your competitors and where you need to work on those aspects where you are not so good.**

You will also come across, as you do your research, products and services that people have indicated they need, which you weren't planning to provide, or situations where what is being provided isn't very good – **these are Opportunities for you**, which you need to consider.

Are these things you should be doing from the start or are they additional products/services you can add at stage two? How will you win time to introduce these new ideas? (See - Time Management below.)

In identifying potential **Threats** during your research it is important to have a contingency plan – the **'What Ifs'** list of questions:

- What will you do if you have an accident or get sick?
- What will you do if a new competitor starts up or an existing competitor drops their prices?
- How can I stop customers or key staff leaving me?

It is no good hoping that it will never happen to you, or not thinking about it until it happens!

TIME MANAGEMENT

In running your own business you will never have enough time. Failure to manage the use of your time could lead to stress and to your business failing.

Part of your time must be spent in activities such as sleeping and eating as well as finding time for family, hobbies or social activities.

The trick is to make the best use of the time you allocate to your business, in other words to concentrate on the essentials – TO PRIORITISE.

Start by asking yourself what you are seeking to achieve **personally** in running your business. **What is the main Aim?**

I want to become very wealthy, I want to provide a good lifestyle for all my family, or whatever.

> **REALLY PRACTICAL TIP The key thing is to write down the Main Aim of your business. Put it on a notice on the wall above where you work to remind yourself every day where you are heading and why you are working so hard.**

That is the Start Point of your Time Management..

Stop and ask yourself whether the thing you are working on at that moment is helping you in achieving your aims – if not, stop doing that and do something that will help. Don't waste time on unimportant things.

A young guy came to see me a few years ago and told me he had a picture of a Mercedes 500 SL on his wall at home, because that's what he was working for, that's what he wanted!

Prioritising

If you can't do everything, make sure you do the most important things – the ones that will contribute towards the success of your business.

Some tasks must be tackled immediately because they are urgent and important (e.g. meeting a deadline). Other tasks are important but do not have to be done so quickly but will get you into trouble if you leave them until it is too late and they are either rushed or else never get done.

You need to divide tasks into three categories:-

Priority A   Must Do - Could mean success or failure

Priority B   Should Do - Will improve performance

Priority C   Could Do - But could be postponed – not vital for survival

Make a List

Sit down each morning or last thing at the end of your business day and make a list of all the things that you have to do, marking whether they are Priority 'A', 'B', or 'C'.

Determine to do the most difficult thing or the most important thing first when you are at your best brain wise.

> **REALLY PRACTICAL TIP As you complete tasks strike them off the list. At the end of the day reward yourself if you have done really well in dealing with a number of key tasks. Remember, you no longer have a boss or anyone telling you what a great job you are doing, so take yourself and your other half out for a meal!**

Procrastination

The main problem is that we tend to put off tasks which seem too difficult or which we do not enjoy – we procrastinate.

Some symptoms of procrastination are:

- **Daydreaming** – thinking about that next holiday – you wish!
- **Allowing interruptions** – come in and have a cup of tea, anything but doing the job!
- **Doing low priority tasks** – tidying up the top of your desk instead of getting on with a 'difficult to deal with' task. Being easily diverted into an 'easy to deal with' non vital task.
- **Taking long breaks** – 'it's my business, I will take a long lunch, I'm the boss.'
- **Constantly finding excuses** – not to do something.

You can deal with procrastination by:

- **Accepting that we all do it** and that it is often caused by fear of failure. This is normal and usually without reason.
- **Disciplining yourself to do it <u>now.</u>**
- **Determining that each piece of paper/e-mail will only be handled once** – when the mail comes in by post or internet – if you can deal with it straightaway do so, even if it is not the most important thing to do at that moment. Add it to your priority list if it can't be dealt with at once. Don't keep on re-visiting mail and then not doing it.
- **Take a part of a really big** project and do it one bit at a time.
  We can eat elephants one bite at a time!!!!
- **Use a 'time management' tool**, on your computer, a diary, wall chart, daily, weekly, monthly planner.
- **Making a list each day of 'Things to Do Today', in order of priority**. Decide how much time to spend on each task and then get on with it.

Time Management Audit

From time to time it would be sensible to just see how you are spending your time, certainly when you are falling behind on work or when you need to win some time to plan a new activity.

You need to keep a log of what you do each day for a short period of time.

To do this draw up some sheets with various headings showing the main things you do each day, e.g., making phone calls, doing the planning for a job, doing the admin., going to visit customers, and doing unimportant things/wasting time.

Down the side of the sheet put half-hourly time periods, e.g. 7.30–8.00 a.m., 8.00–8.30 a.m., and so forth.

Then tick the activity column every half an hour during the day for about ten days to two weeks This will show you how much time you are wasting, or highlight things you are doing which you could delegate to someone else, to free you up to do the things that are best use of your time and will optimise your earning power.

See Chapter 10 - Financial Planning - 'Break Even' to work out how you could afford to employ someone.

Summary - Time Management

- **Start by writing down the Main Aim of your Business and putting it on a large notice to remind you daily of where you are trying to get.**
- **Decide when you will start and finish your working day and stick to it.**
- **Be disciplined in not allowing interruptions, unless they are a 'matter of life or death'.**
- **Finish when you say you are going to, and then shut the door on your business – do not allow it to invade your domestic life.**
- **Work on at least one 'difficult to deal with' task each day and do it when you are at your best.**
- **Handle pieces of paper/e-mails once.**
- **Make a list and strike off tasks as you complete them.**
- **Deal with all your phone calls when you are most likely to catch people in, or on duty.**
- **Don't let the business run you, by failing to manage your time!**
- **Be single minded in the use of your time.**

NETWORKING

It can be very lonely running your own business and it is important therefore to build up a network of contacts who you can call on for advice and support.

It is vital to meet up with other people in business by getting out and attending Business Club meetings and networking with the people there.

There are a number of benefits to 'networking' for your business and you:

- **Mutual support and information through sharing experiences and ideas** – you may meet someone who had the problem you are currently facing and will tell you how they dealt with it.

- **New customers for your services, or suppliers for your business needs** – there is nearly always someone at a meeting who wants your product or service, or knows someone who does.

- **Associates/partners with whom to co-operate on new business ideas or joint ventures** – you have an opportunity to take on a project but don't have all the skills needed, but meet up with someone who is happy to work in association with you, to combine your skills and knowledge.

There are various ways you can build up your network and find out what business gatherings and meetings take place in your area.

- In using an **Accountant, Solicitor or Bank Manager** to help set up aspects of your business you may find that **they attend 'networking' meetings** and will give you the details on how to join in and who to contact.

- **Always ask if you can come along to a meeting to find out what it's like before being persuaded to pay a membership subscription.** That way you can get a good idea of the different opportunities, people, businesses attending without it costing a lot of money.

- Go on to the **Internet** and put in **'business networking'
  and your county/ neighbouring counties** and you will see
  what's available.

The main providers are the local Chambers of Commerce, the
Federation of Small Businesses, the Forum for Private Business,
Business Network International (BNI), Women's Enterprise clubs,
Rotary and Round Table.

- You may belong to a **Professional or Trade Association,**
  so find out if they have meetings in your area.

When you attend a meeting, try to find out from the host whether
there is a list of people attending and what businesses they run. Ask
to be introduced to people on the list who seem fertile ground for
your type of business – this saves going around peering at people's
name badges.

If you go to a meeting (usually a breakfast/lunch occasion) you
will probably start by listening to a speaker. This will give you an
opportunity to discuss the talk with your neighbours which can then
lead to asking them about their business and hopefully, they will ask
you about yours. If they don't tell them anyway!

> **REALLY PRACTICAL TIP Don't just give people
> your business card. They will put it in their wallet
> or top pocket and forget you as soon as they
> have moved on to the next person. Make a point
> of asking for their business card and then follow
> up your face to face meeting with a telephone
> call. Say that you were delighted to meet them at
> the meeting and would welcome the opportunity
> to see them at their business to explore areas
> of mutual interest or to perhaps carry out a free
> audit on some aspects of their business, in which
> you have the experience and expertise.**

You may be invited to give a short presentation of the benefits of your business at Business Club meetings, which should be succinct and bring out what makes you different, the 'benefits' of using you **(known as an 'elevator pitch' - the time you would have in a lift / elevator)**.

At 'meals' type meetings you may be invited to move on to another table after each course, thus enabling you to meet as many people as possible and having to give your presentation at each table. Then, as people get up from the table to circulate you need to make a 'beeline' for the people you would like to talk to for longer.

> **REALLY PRACTICAL TIP** Don't try to carry out your full discussion – save that for when you go to see them – just sell yourself and remember when you then go to see them to be in 'market research' mode. On that first meeting you should not be trying to get a commitment, order, or sale.

SUMMARY

Many people who only deal with other businesses get most of their business in this way.

It is also enjoyable, makes you realise that you are not on your own, and you will find that generally there is a tremendous 'camaraderie' amongst self employed people – **you are, after all individuals against the rest of the world.**

> **REALLY PRACTICAL TIP** Remember also that if your business is not 'business to business', the people you meet at such meetings also have a 'private life' and similar needs to the general public.

OVERALL SUMMARY

Congratulations you've read the book - you have all the pieces of the jigsaw and the basis for making a really great success of your business.

Use all the help that is available starting with talking to a Business Adviser/Counsellor at an Enterprise Agency or a Chamber of Commerce and listening to what they have to tell you.

Have them challenge your Business Plan before you go ahead and then go on talking to them as your business gets underway. Having someone to talk to in those early days and looking from outside-in at your business, will help you see 'the wood from the trees'. Many Agencies offer an ongoing 'Mentoring' service.

KEEP THIS BOOK TO HAND AND LOOK AT IT FROM TIME TO TIME TO REMIND YOU OF THE REALLY PRACTICAL TIPS WHICH WILL SAVE YOU TIME AND TROUBLE.

GOOD LUCK!!

USEFUL CONTACTS / ADDRESSES

- **A.C.A.S. – Employment Guidance**
  www.acas.org.uk
  Tel. 08457 47 47 47

- **Institute of Chartered Accountants England and Wales**
  www.icaew.com
  Tel. 020 7920 8100

- **Institute of Chartered Accountants Scotland**
  www.icas.org
  Tel. 0131 347 0100

- **Institute of Chartered Accountants N. Ireland**
  www.icai.ie
  Tel. 028 9032 160

- **Better Payment Practice Group**
  www.payontime.co.uk

- **British Chambers of Commerce**
  www.britishchambers.org.uk
  Tel. 020 7654 5800

- **British Franchising Association**
  www.thebfa.org
  Tel .01865 379892

- **Companies House**
  www.companieshouse.gov.uk
  Tel. 0870 333 3636

- **Information on Companies, Directorships**
  www.ukdata.com

- **Federation of Small Business (FSB)**
  www.fsb.org.uk
  Tel. 01253 336000

- **Financial Services Authority**
  www.fsa.gov.uk
  Tel. 0845 606 1234

- **Forum of Private Business (FPB)**
  www.fpb.co.uk
  Tel. 01565 634 467

- **Government Statistics**
  www.ons.gov.uk

- **Demographic Statistics**
  www.ons.gov.uk - Click 'People and Places'

- **Health and Safety Executive**
  www.hse.gov.uk
  Tel. 0845 345 0055

- **H.M. Revenue and Customs (Tax, N.I.)**
  www.hmrc.gov.uk
  Tel. O845 915 4515

- **Information Commissioner's Office (Data Protection)**
  www.ico.gov.uk
  Tel. 01625 545 745

- **Institute of Directors**
  www.iod.com
  Tel. 020 7839 1233

- **Intellectual Property**
  www.ipo.gov.uk

- **The Law Society**
  www.lawsociety.org.uk   **'Lawyers for your Business'**
  Tel. 0870 606 2500

- **National Enterprise Network - Enterprise Agencies**
  www.nationalenterprisenetwork.org
  Tel. 01234 831623

- **The Office of Fair Trading**
  www.oft.gov.uk
  Tel. 08457 22 44 99

- **The Chartered Institute of Marketing**
  www.cim.co.uk
  Tel. 01628427500

- **The Patent Office**
  www.ipo.gov.uk
  Tel. 0845 9 500 505

- **Chartered Institute of Personnel and Development**
  www.cipd.co.uk
  Tel. 020 8612 6200

- **The Princes Trust**
  www.princes-trust.org.uk
  Tel. 0800 842 842

- **Shell Livewire**
  www.shell-livewire.org
  Tel. 08457 57 32 52

- **U.K. Trade Fairs and Exhibitions**
  www.exhibitions.co.uk

INDEX

C

D

ACKNOWLEDGEMENTS

I am very grateful to a whole lot of friends and colleagues who have been kind enough to give of their time to read all or parts of the book and to offer their very constructive comments and suggestions.

Firstly my editor Jerry Burman for sharing with me his years of expertise and showing me how to get my words into an end product capable of being published. Thanks to Stephen Ibbitson for introducing me to Jerry.

The following colleagues and good friends for their valuable contributions to the topicality and accuracy of the specialist subjects and for their encouragement.

Jeremy Andrews
Chris Brighton
Andy Cave
George Derbyshire
Judith Ghilks
Stephen Ibbitson
Mike Jennings
Charles Little
Thomas Mott
Luke Mott
Roger Mumby - Croft
Rob Jonckheer
Pauline Steele

ABOUT THE AUTHOR

Kim Hills Spedding has run a business in this field for over 25 years, the first ten years running an Enterprise Agency in Oxford. Many of the suggestions in his book are based on things he and his team did to ensure they provided a sound basis and example for the 3500 businesses they helped start up in Oxfordshire in that time. Since then he has been a self employed independent business advisor/ counsellor/ mentor, giving one to one advice, as well as a trainer presenting Business Planning courses in Berkshire, Bedfordshire, Buckinghamshire, Hertfordshire and Oxfordshire, for both Pre - Start and Existing Businesses, thereby helping many more businesses to start-up and further develop.

Printed in Great Britain
by Amazon